The Scarecrow Author Bibliographies

1. John Steinbeck (Tetsumaro Hayashi). 1973.
2. Joseph Conrad (Theodore G. Ehrsam). 1969.
3. Arthur Miller (Tetsumaro Hayashi). 2d ed. 1976.
4. Katherine Anne Porter (Waldrip & Bauer). 1969.
5. Philip Freneau (Philip M. Marsh). 1970.
6. Robert Greene (Tetsumaro Hayashi). 1971.
7. Benjamin Disraeli (R. W. Stewart). 1972.
8. John Berryman (Richard W. Kelly). 1972.
9. William Dean Howells (Vito J. Brenni). 1973.
10. Jean Anouilh (Kathleen W. Kelly). 1973.
11. E. M. Forster (Alfred Borrello). 1973.
12. The Marquis de Sade (E. Pierre Chanover). 1973.
13. Alain Robbe-Grillet (Dale W. Frazier). 1973.
14. Northrop Frye (Robert D. Denham). 1974.
15. Federico García Lorca (Laurenti & Siracusa). 1974.
16. Ben Jonson (Brock & Welsh). 1974.
17. Four French Dramatists: Eugène Brieux, François de Curel, Emile Fabre, Paul Hervieu (Edmund F. Santa Vicca). 1974.
18. Ralph Waldo Ellison (Jacqueline Covo). 1974.
19. Philip Roth (Bernard F. Rodgers, Jr.). 1974.
20. Norman Mailer (Laura Adams). 1974.
21. Sir John Betjeman (Margaret Stapleton). 1974.
22. Elie Wiesel (Molly Abramowitz). 1974.
23. Paul Laurence Dunbar (Eugene W. Metcalf, Jr.). 1975.
24. Henry James (Beatrice Ricks). 1975.
25. Robert Frost (Lentricchia & Lentricchia). 1976.
26. Sherwood Anderson (Douglas G. Rogers). 1976.
27. Iris Murdoch and Muriel Spark (Tominaga & Schneider-meyer). 1976.
28. John Ruskin (Kirk H. Beetz). 1976.
29. Georges Simenon (Trudee Young). 1976.
30. George Gordon, Lord Byron (Oscar José Santucho). 1976.
31. John Barth (Richard Vine). 1977.
32. John Hawkes (Carol A. Hryciw). 1977.
33. William Everson (Bartlett & Campo). 1977.
34. May Sarton (Lenora Blouin). 1978.
35. Wilkie Collins (Kirk H. Beetz). 1978.
36. Sylvia Plath (Lane & Stevens). 1978.
37. E. B. White (A. J. Anderson). 1978.
38. Henry Miller (Lawrence J. Shifreen). 1979.
39. Ralph Waldo Emerson (Jeanetta Boswell). 1979.
40. James Dickey (Jim Elledge). 1979.
41. Henry Fielding (H. George Hahn). 1979.
42. Paul Goodman (Tom Nicely). 1979.
43. Christopher Marlowe (Kenneth Friedenreich). 1979.
44. Leo Tolstoy (Egan & Egan). 1979.
45. T. S. Eliot (Beatrice Ricks). 1980.
46. Allen Ginsberg (Michelle P. Kraus). 1980.
47. Anthony Burgess (Jeutonne P. Brewer). 1980.
48. Tennessee Williams (Drewey Wayne Gunn). 1980.

ANTHONY BURGESS

A Bibliography

by Jeutonne Brewer

*(with a Foreword by
Anthony Burgess)*

(Scarecrow Author Bibliographies, No. 47)

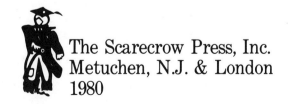

The Scarecrow Press, Inc.
Metuchen, N.J. & London
1980

To my parents,
William Louis Patten
and
Ila May Patten

Library of Congress Cataloging in Publication Data

Brewer, Jeutonne, 1939-
    Anthony Burgess : a bibliography.

    (Scarecrow author bibliographies ; no. 47)
    Includes indexes.
    1. Burgess, Anthony, 1917-   --Bibliography.
Z8132.2.B73   [PR6052.U638]   016.823'914   80-413
ISBN 0-8108-1286-X

Copyright © 1980 by Jeutonne P. Brewer

Manufactured in the United States of America

TABLE OF CONTENTS

Foreword by Anthony Burgess   v

Introduction   viii

Chronology   xiii

I.   Works by Anthony Burgess   1
     A.   Novels   3
     B.   Short Stories   31
     C.   Poems   32
     D.   Non-Fiction Books, Sections of Books   33
     E.   Works Translated   44
     F.   Works Edited   46
     G.   Articles, Essays, and Reviews   49
     H.   Interviews   117
     I.   Recordings   122

II. Works about Anthony Burgess   123
     J.   Books, Sections of Books   125
     K.   Dissertations   130
     L.   Articles and Essays   132
     M.   Bibliographies   147

Late Additions   149

Name Index   151

Title Index   157

Index to Names and Titles in Works by
     Anthony Burgess   166

iii

FOREWORD TO A BIBLIOGRAPHY

I am filled with various emotions when I consider this
work to which I prepend a brief blessing, but the chief ones
are wonder and anger. I genuinely admire and wonder at the
industry that has gone into the compiling of this bibliography;
I also wonder at the ingenuity whereby so many pieces of fu-
gitive writing have been tracked down (I would not have known
how or where to start); I wonder at the amount of work I
seem to have done in the last twenty-odd years, knowing that
this bibliography cannot ever have hoped to catalogue it all.
For there have been odd jobs done in Australasia and the Far
East. The noted heterosexual magazine Queen, for which I
worked as music critic, has buried my writings under furs
and lingerie. The music I have written, for stage, film, and
concert hall, cannot properly enter here, but it was work and
hard work. Yet not so hard as the hard work of writing.

This is where my anger comes in. It seems to me
wrong that one should have had to do so much writing in order
to make a living, and not a very good living at that. I write
these lines in Monaco, where the blue waters are totally obscured by the yachts that are anchored there. Not one of
these yachts belongs to a man or woman who writes or has
written. The nearest writer's yacht is at Cannes, and it belongs to Harold Robbins, the well-known carpetbagger, who,
publicly proclaiming himself the greatest living writer, is

v

probably not really a writer at all. I mean that he does not
seem to struggle with words. He sets up puppets who rage
and lunge at each other, but the language is very flaccid.
There is a real writer at Antibes, Graham Greene, who, at
75, lives in a very small apartment overlooking the traffic
and, beyond, more non-writers' yachts, and still appears to
worry about money.

I am not angry enough to wish to give up writing for
a living, even if my financial situation allowed it, but I am
angry at not having been able to concentrate on the production of novels. To some extent I blame myself for having
done so much reviewing, but, when any journal sends me a
book unsolicited for review, I find it easier to write the review than to send the book back. It is also hard to say no
to a request for an article or a preface or an interview. All
writers are superstitious and fear that if they say no once
they may never be asked again. The money from occasional
writings is small, but it is real and immediate and pays
grocery bills. It also bears a direct relation to the amount
of work put into an article, whereas the financial rewards of
fiction have been, for me, pretty inadequate. Moreover, as
one gets deeper into the fictional art one realises that one
is bound to produce less and less marketable work: there is
too much interest in the manipulation of language, symbolist
trickery, human character, and the public does not require
any of this.

But to return to the bibliography and not to its causa-
tive organisms. It is going to have a value for me quite
different from any value it may have for students of the state
of British fiction in the late twentieth century. For many of
the pieces, in their mere titles, recall vividly the occasion

of writing. There is an article written for <u>The Listener</u> about the Profumo scandal, and it was a difficult article to write. I started it at ten at night and finished it at dawn, just in time to put it on the train from Etchingham, East Sussex (a few miles from Batemans, Kipling's old home), to Charing Cross, London, where a runner was waiting to pick it up. It was a glorious summer dawn, and I looked out at my garden to see that my fifteen guinea pigs had chewed through the wire netting of their cage and were running all around. I had to get down there to recorral them. I remember the occasion, but I do not remember the date. Now, with this bibliography before me, I can place it exactly--one week before--now where the devil, somewhere in June nineteen-sixty-something--oh, never mind. Later. It's there, fixed forever, that is the important point.

My gratitude, then, to Professor Brewer, who has done a remarkable job. This is what Aldous Huxley would call the logarithm of two score years of overproduction. But no one can be said to overproduce who has a wife and a child to support. Writing may be an art, but it is also a trade. If we define art as disinterested endeavour which meets little material reward, then this art of bibliography must be very great indeed. And, in the hands of Professor Brewer, it is.

Anthony Burgess
Monte Carlo
June 1979

INTRODUCTION

Musician, linguist, novelist, critic, editor, translator--these are all the roles of one individual, John Anthony Burgess Wilson. Each of these areas has influenced and is reflected in his writing, his experiences as musician, linguist, and writer being important recurring elements in his novels. One must study in detail his use of language, of musical patterns, and of satire and absurdity in order to understand Anthony Burgess the writer.

During the decades covered by this bibliography Burgess wrote more than two dozen novels, in addition to critical works, books about language, Shakespeare, and Hemingway, and over four hundred articles and reviews. Burgess also found time to translate and edit other works. In fact, the reader finds it difficult to read as fast as Burgess publishes; the critic finds it difficult to digest his work, because of both its scope and its quantity.

Burgess did not turn to writing as a profession until his forties. After serving in the military in World War II, he returned to England and taught at Birmingham University, lectured in phonetics for the Ministry of Education, and taught at Banbury School in Oxfordshire. Answering an advertisement in the Times Educational Supplement, Burgess applied for a teaching position on the Channel Island of Sark. He later discovered that he had mistakenly applied for a position in Malaya. Before leaving England, he submitted A

Vision of Battlements to Heinemann, who agreed to publish the book, but only as a second novel. Burgess then wrote The Worm and the Ring and submitted it to the publisher. It was rejected, because it was "too Catholic and too guilt-ridden. " In 1954 Burgess accepted the teaching position, error or not, and went to Malaya. There he taught English and learned first-hand about the complex Malayan culture, his experiences being reflected in his first three published novels, Time for a Tiger (1956), The Enemy in the Blanket (1958), and Beds in the East (1959). Throughout this early period, or first career, Burgess also pursued his serious interest in music, writing chamber pieces and symphonies.

Returning to England in 1959, Burgess was released from the Colonial Service. Doctor's diagnosis--brain tumor. Although the suspected tumor ended his career with the Colonial Service, it sparked a new career; given a year to live, he set out to write a legacy for his wife, producing five novels in one year. The dark days of illness even provided Burgess with the material for a novel, The Doctor Is Sick, in which a linguist with a suspected brain tumor experiences London's seamier side when he escapes from the hospital.

The danger of illness receded, but Burgess's penchant for writing did not. The flow of novels and other publications continued. The quantity of Burgess's work is often referred to in reviews of his books. Burgess has defended his prolificacy by pointing out that it is not unusual in the history of literature. Furthermore, he has the ability to work long hours. Because he is a dedicated, determined and talented writer, keeping a bibliography of his works current is an exercise in frustration.

Burgess introduced early in his writing career an

onomastic maze for the student of his works. He published
his first three novels, about British colonialism in Malaya,
under the name "Anthony Burgess" in order to escape censure; the Colonial Service disapproved of its officers' ex-
pressing anti-colonial attitudes. Leaving the Colonial Service
did not end Burgess's need for a pseudonym. Following the
advice of his publisher, he used the name "Joseph Kell" to
hide his prolificness from the critics. In 1961 Burgess's
Devil of a State and The Worm and the Ring and Joseph
Kell's One Hand Clapping were published; in 1963 Burgess's
Honey for the Bears and Kell's Inside Mr. Enderby. Sand-
wiched between these novels were two others, A Clockwork
Orange and The Wanting Seed, both published in 1962 under
the name Anthony Burgess. "John Burgess Wilson" published
English Literature in 1958 and Language Made Plain in 1965.

In addition to the quantity and scope of Burgess's work
and his use of pseudonyms are the usual transatlantic problems for the bibliographer--different titles for the same book
on each side of the Atlantic and simultaneous publication of
a book in England and America. For example, A Malayan
Trilogy became The Long Day Wanes in the United States,
and Here Comes Everybody became Re Joyce.

The quantity and quality of Burgess's writing demand
a comprehensive bibliography. Academic critics are increas-
ingly concerned with his work, as the Special Session on
Burgess at the 1978 meeting of the Modern Language Association attests. This bibliography is offered to fill an obvious
gap in the constantly expanding literature by and about Burgess, to provide a source of information for Burgess students, both those of the present and those of the future.

Because Burgess is an energetic and productive writer
this bibliography can be only transitorily complete; it is a

source of information rather than a memorial. I decided early in my collecting and organizing efforts that this work would be eclectic rather than selective. References to his writings were often brief in earlier criticism and collections, but this glimmer of recognition of Burgess the novelist and critic is part of the record. Burgess's readers often have responded to his articles and letters; this correspondence typically extends over several weeks or months, with Burgess sometimes adding his clarifying or opposing replies to readers' letters. I have included letters by the unknown as well as by well-known authors and academics. I have listed these materials in the appropriate sections, cross-referencing them so that the user of the bibliography can trace the ideas and opinions about language and literature.

Reviews of Burgess's works are listed under the work reviewed. Some reviewers provide analyses of the Burgess canon in addition to the review of a current work. These reviews, properly considered criticism, are also cited in the section on articles and essays about Burgess. In these cases I have cross-referenced the listings.

There remains the pleasant task of acknowledging the help I received during the preparation of this manuscript. I owe thanks to Marie B. Bullard, librarian at the Walter Clinton Jackson Library, for helping me locate and obtain copies of many of the materials included in this book. At one point my requests skewed her accounting of materials loaned and borrowed; she correctly identified the culprit, but continued her efficient efforts to locate materials for me. I also appreciate Marcie Kingsley's help in tracking down Burgess's review of "Joseph Kell's" Inside Mr. Enderby.

Mary Bullington and Deborah Mutnick, graduate research

assistants, spent many hours checking sources, while maintaining their good humor during the searching process. Without their help in the early stages of collecting and organizing the material this project would have been much less enjoyable. I owe thanks to Ian Abrams for his help in using the computer as an efficient aid in preparing the manuscript, especially for supervising the process of putting the material into the machine. Doris Hardie also deserves a note of thanks for willingly learning the process and helping to enter the material and edit the manuscript. Anyone who has spent even a few hours at the keyboard of a little screen interactive terminal will realize the importance of their contribution. Without their help this project would have been much more tedious.

I owe a special note of thanks to Marlene Pratto of the Academic Computer Center. She encouraged us in our efforts to use the computer, coached us through our difficulties, and cheered with us in our successes. Her help in devising the method of compiling the index deserves more recognition than this brief note of thanks can provide.

I wish to thank the Research Council of the University of North Carolina at Greensboro for a grant that helped defray the costs of preparing this manuscript.

Finally, I owe thanks and gratitude to Chris Brewer for his generous patience and encouragement during yet another project.

J. P. B.
Greensboro, N. C.
January 1979

CHRONOLOGY

1917 Born February 25, 1917, in Manchester, England, into an Augustinian Catholic Lancashire family. Son of Joseph Wilson, a pianist, and Elizabeth Burgess Wilson, a musical comedy actress known as "Beautiful Belle Burgess."

1918 Death of his mother and only sister during the influenza epidemic; brought up by an Irish stepmother.

1940 Awarded the B. A. degree with honors from Manchester University; specialized in English.

1940- Served in the British Army Education Corps as musical director of a special services unit entertaining troops in Europe; discharged with the rank of sergeant-major.
1946

1942 Marriage to Llewela Isherwood Jones.

1946- Education officer for the Central Advisory Council for Adult Education in the Forces. Lecturer at Birmingham University.
1948

1948- Lecturer in phonetics for the Ministry of Education.
1950

1950- Master, Banbury Grammar School, Oxfordshire.
1954

1953 Answered an advertisement in the Times Educational Supplement to teach on the Channel Island of Sark; later discovered that by mistake he had applied to teach in Malaya.

1954 A Vision of Battlements rejected as a first novel, although acceptable as a second novel; The Worm

xiii

and the Ring then rejected as "too Catholic and too guilt-ridden. "

1954-
1957
Senior Lecturer in English, Malayan Teachers Training College, Khata Baru, Malaya.

1956
Publication of Time for a Tiger; used a pseudonym, "Anthony Burgess, " to avoid censure from the Colonial Service for expression of anti-colonial attitudes.

1957-
1960
English Language Specialist, Education Department, Brunei, Borneo.

1958
Publication, as "John Burgess Wilson, " of English Literature: A Survey for Students; publication, as "Anthony Burgess, " of The Enemy in the Blanket.

1959
Publication, as "Anthony Burgess, " of Beds in the East.

1960
The Right to an Answer; The Doctor Is Sick.

1961
Devil of a State; The Worm and the Ring; One Hand Clapping, as "Joseph Kell. "

1962
The Wanting Seed; A Clockwork Orange.

1963
Inside Mr. Enderby, as "Joseph Kell"; Honey for the Bears; The Novel Today.

1964
Nothing Like the Sun; The Eve of Saint Venus.

1965
Here Comes Everybody (entitled Re Joyce in the U.S.); Language Made Plain; A Vision of Battlements.

1966
Tremor of Intent.

1967
A Shorter Finnegans Wake; The Novel Now.

1968
Wife Llewela died. Burgess married Lilana Macellari, daughter of Contessa Lucrezia Pasi della Pergoli. Left England to live on island of Malta; involuntary expatriate because of the high taxes Britain imposes upon writers. Enderby, comprising Inside Mr. Enderby and Enderby Outside; Urgent Copy.

1969-   Elected Fellow, Royal Society of Literature; Writer-
1970   in-Residence, University of North Carolina.

1970-   Professor, Columbia University; Visiting Fellow,
1971   Princeton University.

1970   Shakespeare.

1971   MF; Stanley Kubrick's film version of A Clockwork
        Orange awarded the New York Film Critics Award.

1972-   Literary Adviser, Guthrie Theatre, Minneapolis,
1975   Minnesota.

1972-   Distinguished Professor, City College, New York.
1973

1972   Joysprick

1973   Sixth Annual Award in Literature, National Arts
        Club; Obscenity and the Arts.

1974   The Clockwork Testament, or Enderby's End; Na-
        poleon Symphony.

1976   Beard's Roman Women; A Long Trip to Teatime;
        New York.

1977   Abba Abba; L'Homme de Nazareth; the television
        production of Jesus of Nazareth.

1978   Ernest Hemingway and His World; 1985.

Works by

Anthony Burgess

A. NOVELS

A01 ABBA ABBA

London: Faber, 1977.

Reviews:
Amis, M. New Statesman, 17 June 1977, pp. 821-22.
Driver, C. J. "Dying to Be Told." Guardian Weekly, 12 June 1977, p. 12.
Listener, 2 June 1977, p. 729.
Morgan, Edwin. "The Thing's the Thing." Times Literary Supplement, 3 June 1977, p. 669.
Observer, 29 May 1977, p. 28.
Observer, 26 June 1977, p. 29.
Observer, 18 December 1977, p. 21.
Observer, 25 February 1979, p. 37.
Paulin, T. Encounter, 49 (October 1977), pp. 82-85.
Publishers' Weekly, 29 January 1979, p. 112.
Ricks, Christopher. "The Abracadabra Man." Sunday Times (London), 29 May 1977, p. 41.
Schneider, Rupert. "A Small Brilliance." Canadian Forum, 57 (March 1978), p. 34.
Scott, P. Country Life, 30 June 1977, pp. 1849-50.
Sunday Times (London), 29 May 1977, p. 41.
Times (London), 2 June 1977, p. 9.

A02 BEARD'S ROMAN WOMEN

New York: McGraw-Hill, 1976. Photos by David Robinson.
London: Hutchinson, 1977.

Reviews:
Adams, P. -L. Atlantic, October 1976, p. 114.
America, 2 October 1976, p. 196.
Booklist, 1 September 1976, p. 22.

Economist, 26 February 1977, p. 117.
Illustrated London News, April 1977, p. 59.
Kirkus Reviews, 1 July 1976, pp. 747-48.
Korn, E. Times Literary Supplement, 11 February 1977, p. 145.
Lodge, David. New Statesman, 11 February 1977, pp. 194-95.
Moynahan, J. New York Times Book Review, 10 October 1976, p. 8.
Murray, John. Best Sellers, 36 (March 1977), p. 379.
Newsweek, 25 October 1976, pp. 110-11.
Observer, 6 February 1977, p. 31.
Observer, 26 June 1977, p. 29.
Observer, 18 December 1977, p. 21.
Pritchard, W. H. Hudson Review, 30 (Spring 1977), 147-60.
Publishers Weekly, 19 July 1976, p. 130.
Ricks, Christopher. "Faces in the Mirror." Sunday Times (London), 6 February 1977, p. 41.
Rogers, Pat. "On the Move." Spectator, 12 February 1977, p. 23.
Soete, M. Library Journal, August 1976, p. 1656.
Tennant, Emma. "Burgess's Many Voices." Listener, 10 February 1977, p. 189.
Theroux, Paul. "Angry Old Burgess." Guardian Weekly, 20 February 1977, p. 22.
Times Literary Supplement, 24 February 1977, p. 12.
Virginia Quarterly Review, 53 (Summer 1977), p. ciii.
Wade, Rosalind. Contemporary Review, 230 (April 1977), pp. 213-17.
West Coast Review of Books, 3 (January 1977), p. 25.
Woods, M. New York Review of Books, 30 September 1976, pp. 40-42.
World Literature Today, 51 (Summer 1977), pp. 618-19.

A03   BEDS IN THE EAST

London: Heinemann, 1959.
London: Heinemann, 1964. Reprint.
London: Heinemann, 1968. Reissue.

Reviews:
Smith, Peter Duval. New Statesman, 9 May 1959, pp. 663-64.

A04 A CLOCKWORK ORANGE

London: Heinemann, 1962.
New York: Norton, 1963. paper.
London: Pan, 1964. paper.
New York: Ballantine, 1965. paper.
New York: Ballantine, 1971. paper.

Translations:
Belmont, George, and Hortense Charbrier, trans. L'Orange mécanique [French]. Paris: Laffont, 1972.
Bossi, Floriana, trans. Un'Arancia a Orologeria [Italian]. Torino: Einaudi, 1969.
_____, trans. Un'Arancia a Orologeria [Italian]. Torino: Einaudi, 1972.
Brumm, Walter, trans. Uhrwerk Orange [German]. München: Heyne, 1972.
Gress, Elsa, trans. A Clockwork Orange [Danish]. [?]: Bramsen and Hjort, 1972.
Leal, Aníbal, trans. La naranja mecánica [Spanish]. 2nd ed. Coleccion Metamorfosis. Buenos Aires: Minotauro, 1971.
_____, trans. La naranja mecánica [Spanish]. 4th ed. Buenos Aires: Minotauro, 1973.
_____, trans. La naranja mecánica [Spanish]. 7th ed. Buenos Aires: Ed. Minotauro, 1973.
Lundgren, Caj. En Apelsin med Urverk [Swedish]. Stockholm: Wahlström and Widstrand, 1972.
Shin'ichiro, Inui, trans. Tokei Jikake No Orenji [Japanese]. Tokyo: Hayakawa Shobo, 1971.
Üstel, Aziz, trans. Otamatik portakal [Turkish]. Ankara: Bilgi Yayinevi, 1973.
Zivković, Zoran, trans. Paklena pomorandža. Beograd: Beogradski izdavacko-graficki zavod, 1973.

Reviews:
Bergonzi, Bernard. "Funny Book." New York Review of Books, 20 May 1965, p. 16.
Best Sellers, 1 October 1965, p. 274.
Bordwell, H. Today, 23 (January 1968), p. 30.

Davis, Robert Gorham. "The Perilous Balance."
Hudson Review, 16 (Summer 1963), pp. 281-89.
Hicks, Granville. "Fertile World of Anthony Bur-
gess." Saturday Review, 15 July 1967, p. 28.
Same as [L60].
Josselson, Diana. Kenyon Review, 25, No. 3 (Sum-
mer 1963), pp. 559-60.
Levin, Martin. New York Times Book Review, 7
April 1963, p. 36.
Moran, John F. Library Journal, 15 February
1963, p. 793.
New Leader, 7 January 1963, p. 22.
People's World (San Francisco), 22 June 1963, p.
5.
Schickel, Richard. Show, 3 (August 1963), pp. 38-
40.
Talbot, David. New Herald Tribune Books, 14
April 1963, p. 7.
Taubman, Robert. "Djunaesque." New Statesman,
18 May 1962, pp. 717-18.
Time, 15 February 1963, p. 103.
Times Literary Supplement, 25 May 1962, p. 377.
Walters, Raymond, Jr. "Say It with Paperbacks."
New York Times Book Review, 4 December
1966, p. 60.

A05   A CLOCKWORK ORANGE [Film]. By Stanley Kubrick.
Based on the novel by Anthony Burgess.

New York: Abelard-Schuman, 1972.
New York: Ballantine, 1972. paper.

Reviews:
Alpert, Hollis. "Milk-Plus and Ultra Violence."
Saturday Review, 25 December 1971, pp. 40-41,
60.
Austin, Charles M. "Stirring the Guttywuts."
Christian Century, 15 February 1972, p. 207.
Burgess, Anthony. "Burgess on Kubrick on 'Clock-
work.'" Library Journal, 1 May 1973, p. 1506.
Same as [G52].
Choice, October 1973, p. 1207.
Ciglic, M. "Mechanicna oranza." EKran, 11,
Nos. 104-105 (1973), pp. 158-67.
Commonweal, 14 January 1972, pp. 351-52.
Commonweal, 14 July 1972, pp. 383-86.

Comuzio, E. "Ludwig Van e gli altri." Cine-
forum, No. 119 (January 1973), pp. 75-78.
Daniels, D. "A Clockwork Orange." Sight and
Sound, 42, No. 1 (Winter 1972-1973), pp. 44-46.
Denby, David. "Pop Nihilism at the Movies."
Atlantic, March 1972, pp. 100-04.
Frezzato, A. "Riproposta della vita." Cineforum,
No. 119 (January 1973), pp. 66-74.
Gambetti, G. "Due tipi de violenza." Cineforum,
No. 119 (January 1973), pp. 54-65.
Grumenik, Arthur. "A Clockwork Orange: Novel
into Film." Film Heritage, 7, No. 4 (Summer
1972), pp. 7-18.
Hatch, Robert. Nation, 3 January 1972, pp. 27-28.
Hiltmen, E. "Kenelle kellopeli soi." Filmhillu,
No. 4 (1973), pp. 20-22.
Hughes, Robert. Time, 27 December 1971, p. 59.
Jackson, Burgess. Film Quarterly, 25, No. 3
(Spring 1972), pp. 33-36.
Kael, Pauline. "Stanley Strangelove." New Yorker,
1 January 1972, pp. 50-53.
Kaufmann, Stanley. New Republic, 1 January 1972,
pp. 22, 32.
Kellogg, Jean. "The Cineast as Moralizer."
Christian Century, 6 September 1972, p. 878.
Khanuitin, I. "Koshmart na bdesheto." Kinoizkustvo,
28 (September 1973), pp. 50-63.
"Kubrick Country." Int. Penelope Houston. Satur-
day Review, 25 December 1971, pp. 42-43.
Mamber, S. "A Clockwork Orange." Cinema
(U.S.), 7, No. 3 (1972), pp. 48-57.
Marszalek, R. "Help!" Kino, 8 (June 1973),
pp. 42-49.
Pechter, William S. "Peckinpah and Kubrick: Fire
and Ice." Commentary, 53 (March 1972), pp.
79-82.
Ricks, Christopher. New York Review of Books,
6 April 1972, pp. 28-31.
Samuels, Charles Thomas. "The Context of A
Clockwork Orange." American Scholar, 4 (Sum-
mer 1972), pp. 439-43.
Sarivonova, M. "Konfrontatsiia--Varsheva 73."
Kinoizkustvo, 28 (August 1973), pp. 69-75.
Shickel, Richard. Life, 4 February 1972, p. 14.
Simonelli, G. "Arancia meccanica." Cschedario,
No. 62 (February 1973), pp. 53-63.
Strick, Philip. "Kubrick's Horrorshow." Sight

and Sound, 41 (Winter 1971-72), pp. 44-46.
Time, 20 December 1971, pp. 80-81, 85.
Zimmerman, Paul D. "Kubrick's Brilliant Vision."
Newsweek, 3 January 1972, pp. 28-33.

A06 A CLOCKWORK ORANGE AND HONEY FOR THE
BEARS

New York: Modern Library, 1968.

A07 THE CLOCKWORK TESTAMENT; OR ENDERBY'S END

London: Hart-Davis, MacGibbon, 1974.
New York: Knopf, 1975. Illus. by the Quays.
New York: Bantam, 1976.

Last of the Enderby series; see also Enderby [A10],
Enderby Outside [A11] and Inside Mr. Enderby [A16].

Translations:
Brumm, Walter, trans. Das Uhrwerk-Testament
[German]. München: Heyne, 1974.
Le Testament de l'orange [French]. Paris: Laffont,
1975.

Reviews:
Adams, Phoebe. Atlantic, February 1975, p. 122.
Allen, Bruce. Library Journal, 15 January 1975,
p. 144.
America, 26 April 1975, p. 320.
Book World, 9 March 1975, p. 1.
Book World, 30 May 1976, Sect. F, p. 8.
Booklist, 1 March 1975, p. 669.
Broyard, Anatole. "Poetry Can Kill a Man." New
York Times, 1 February 1975, p. 25.
Byatt, A. S. "All Life Is One." Times (London),
6 June 1974, p. 8.
_____. Times (London), 28 November 1974, p.
4.
Economist, 8 June 1974, p. 107.
Edwards, T. New York Review of Books, 20
February 1975, p. 34.
Foote, Timothy. Time, 17 March 1975, p. 84, 86.
Guardian Weekly, 22 June 1974, p. 22.
Guardian Weekly, 28 December 1974, p. 6.

Harper's, May 1975, p. 55.
Kirkus Reviews, 1 December 1974, p. 1266.
Koltz, Newton. America, 22 March 1975, p. 215.
Lhamon, W. T. New Republic, 22 February 1975, p. 29.
Murray, John J. Best Sellers, 1 March 1975, p. 523.
National Observer, 1 February 1975, p. 21.
New Yorker, 10 March 1975, p. 118-19.
Nicol, Charles. National Review, 9 May 1975, p. 521.
Nye, Robert. Christian Science Monitor, 25 April 1975, p. 27.
Observer, 2 June 1974, p. 33.
O'Hara, J. D. New York Times Book Review, 2 February 1975, p. 4.
Ostermann, R. National Observer, 1 February 1975, p. 21.
Prescott, P. S. Newsweek, 7 April 1975, p. 89.
Prince, Peter. New Statesman, 21 June 1974, p. 894.
Pritchard, William. Listener, 13 June 1974, p. 776-77.
Publishers Weekly, 2 December 1974, p. 57.
Publishers Weekly, 19 January 1976, p. 104.
Raban, Jonathan. "What Shall We Do About Anthony Burgess?" Encounter, 43 (November 1974), 83-88. Same as [L97].
Rabinowitz, Dorothy. Saturday Review, 25 January 1975, p. 44.
Smith, Godfrey. Sunday Times (London), 2 June 1974, p. 40.
Sunday Times (London), 21 July 1974, p. 31.
Sunday Times (London), 1 December 1974, p. 40.
Times Literary Supplement, 7 June 1974, p. 601.

A08   DEVIL OF A STATE

London: Heinemann, 1961.
New York: Norton, 1962.
New York: Ballantine, 1968. paper.
New York: Norton, 1975. paper.

Reviews:
Gross, John. "La Noia." New Statesman, 24 November 1961, pp. 801-02.

Jebb, Julian. Time and Tide, 2 November 1961, p. 1850.

Jennings, Elizabeth. Listener, 28 December 1961, p. 1133.

Keown, Eric. Punch, 15 November 1961, pp. 730-31.

Kirkus Service, 1 November 1961, p. 979.

Levin, Martin. New York Times Book Review, 25 February 1962, p. 40.

Mitchell, Julian. "Wracks of Empire." Spectator, 3 November 1961, p. 636.

_____. Weekly Review, 9 November 1961, pp. 9-12.

Price, Martin. "Bands of the Human Spectrum." Saturday Review, 17 March 1962, pp. 27-28.

Publishers Weekly, 11 December 1967, p. 48.

Quigley, Isabel. Guardian, 10 November 1961, p. 6.

Rogers, W. G. New York Herald Tribune Books, 4 March 1962, p. 13.

Springfield Republican, 11 March 1962, Sect. D, p. 4.

Times Literary Supplement, 17 November 1961, p. 829.

A09 THE DOCTOR IS SICK

London: Heinemann, 1960.
New York: Norton, 1960.
London: Pan, 1963. paper.
New York: Norton, 1966.
New York: Ballantine, 1967. paper.

Translations:
  Lundgren, Caj, trans. Doktorn är sjuk [Swedish].
    Stockholm: Wahlström and Widstrand, 1974.
  Uusitalo, Inkere, trans. Pipopää Potilas [Finnish].
    Hämeenlinna: A. A. Karisto, 1973.
  Wiskott, Inge, trans. Der Doktor ist Übergesch-
    nappt [German]. Tübingen: Erdmann, 1968.
  _____, trans. Der Doktor ist Übergeschnappt
    [German]. Reinbek bei Hamburg: Rowohlt, 1970.

Reviews:
  Baumbach, Elinor. "Professor's Pajama Games."
    Saturday Review, 7 May 1966, p. 95.

Books and Bookmen, 17 (August 1972) p. 11.
Bowen, John. "A Matter of Concern." Time and Tide, 26 November 1960, p. 1445.
Choice, 3 (July-August 1966), pp. 407-08.
Donoghue, Denis. New York Review of Books, 9 June 1966, p. 20.
Fleischer, L. Publishers Weekly, 6 February 1967, p. 77.
Grigson, Geoffrey. "Four Fantasies." Spectator, 25 November 1960, p. 860.
Hicks, Granville. "Fertile World of Anthony Burgess." Saturday Review, 15 July 1968, p. 28. Same as [L60].
Keeney, Willard. "Ripeness Is All: Late, Late Romanticism and Other Recent Fiction." Southern Review, N. S. 3 (October 1967), pp. 1050-61.
Kirkus Service, 1 March 1966, p. 266.
Lindroth, J. B. America, 30 April 1966, p. 630.
Malin, Irving. Commonweal, 20 May 1966, pp. 260-61.
Maloff, Saul. New York Times Book Review, 24 April 1966, p. 5.
Ostermann, R. National Observer, 9 May 1966, p. 25.
Punch, 21 December 1960, p. 909.
Ready, William. "But the Patient Is Fine." Critic, 25, No. 2 (October-November 1966), pp. 114-16.
Richardson, Maurice. New Statesman, 3 December 1960, p. 888.
_____. Punch, 21 December 1960, p. 909.
_____. Times Literary Supplement, 23 December 1960, p. 825.
Rosofsky, H. L. Library Journal, 1 April 1966, p. 1920.
Time, 29 April 1966, p. 114.
West, Paul. "Diction Addiction." Book Week, 15 May 1966, p. 14.

A10   ENDERBY

New York: Norton, 1968.
New York: Ballantine, 1969. paper.

Comprising Inside Mr. Enderby [A16] and Enderby Outside [A11].

Translations:
Bossi, Floriana, trans. La dolce bestia [Italian].
[Torino]: Einaudi, 1972.

Reviews:
Baxter, Ralph C. Best Sellers, 15 June 1968,
  p. 126.
Bergonzi, Bernard. "A Poet's Life." Hudson
  Review, 21 (Winter 1968-69), pp. 764-68.
Booklist, 15 July 1968, p. 1263.
Broadwater, Bowden. "A Glob and His Guts."
  Book World, 9 June 1968, p. 13.
Choice, 5-6 (July-August 1968), p. 620.
Coleman, J. Observer, 26 May 1968, p. 29.
Curley, Dorothy. Library Journal, 1 June 1968,
  pp. 2257-58.
Davenport, Guy. National Review, 18 June 1968,
  p. 613, 615.
DeMott, Benjamin. "Gog into Vision." New York
  Times Book Review, 30 June 1968, pp. 5, 34.
Hicks, Granville. "Poetry and Defense." Saturday
  Review, 8 June 1968, pp. 37-38.
Kirkus Reviews, 1 April 1968, p. 415.
McDowell, Frederick W. P. "Recent British Fic-
  tion: Some Established Writers." Contemporary
  Literature, 11 (Summer 1970), pp. 401-48.
Malin, Irving. Commonweal, 15 November 1968,
  pp. 262-63.
Mablekos, Carole. Survey of Contemporary Liter-
  ature, Vol. 4, 1977, p. 2255.
Masterplots Annual, 1969, p. 115.
Morris, Robert K. "The Flatulent Poet." Nation,
  22 July 1968, p. 58.
New York Times, 11 June 1968, p. 45.
New Yorker, 29 June 1968, pp. 87-88.
O'Malley, Michael. "Bid and Made." Critic, 22,
  No. 2 (October-November 1968), pp. 95-99.
Ostermann, R. National Observer, 24 June 1968,
  p. 19.
Pettingell, Phoebe. "The Boor Joyce." New
  Leader, 9 September 1968, pp. 20-21.
Price, R. G. Punch, 29 May 1968, p. 794.
Pritchard, William H. "Burgess vs. Scholes."
  Novel, 2 (1969), pp. 164-67.
Publishers Weekly, 1 April 1968, p. 34.
Publishers Weekly, 4 August 1969, p. 50.
Rees, D. Encounter, 31 (October 1968), p. 74.

Reynolds, S. New Statesman, 31 May 1968, p. 735.
Shrapnel, N. Manchester Guardian Weekly, 6 June
1968, p. 11.
Solotaroff, Theodore. "The Busy Hand of Burgess."
New Republic, 22 August 1968, pp. 20-22.
Tannenbaum, Earl. Library Journal, 1 June 1968,
p. 2257.
Time, 14 June 1968, p. 93.
Times Literary Supplement, 30 May 1968, p. 545.
Waugh, Auberon. "Seat of Pleasure." Spectator,
31 May 1968, p. 745.
Wain, John. New York Review of Books, 22
August 1968, p. 34.

A11 ENDERBY OUTSIDE

London: Heinemann, 1968.
Harmondsworth: Penguin, 1971. paper.

Reviews:
Aggeler, Geoffrey. "Mr. Enderby and Mr. Burgess." Malahat Review, 10 (April 1969),
pp. 104-10.
Green, Martin. Month, 40 (November 1968),
pp. 286-87.
Holmes, Richard. Times (London), 1 June 1968,
p. 20.
Nowell, Robert. "Horror Show." Tablet, 25 May
1968, pp. 529-30.
Observer, 15 August 1971, p. 18.
Rees, Davis. "Heroes of Our Time." Encounter,
31 (October 1968), pp. 74-76.

See also Enderby [A10].

A12 THE ENEMY IN THE BLANKET

London: Heinemann, 1958.
London: Heinemann, 1964. Reprint.
London: Heinemann, 1968. Reissued.

Included in A Malayan Trilogy [A20] and The Long
Day Wanes [A18].

A13   THE EVE OF SAINT VENUS

London: Sidgwick and Jackson, 1964.   Illus. by
    Edward Pagram.
Rexdale, Ontario: Ambassador, 1964.
New York: Norton, 1967.
London: New English Library, 1968.
New York: Norton, 1970. Illus. by Edward Pagram.
New York: Ballantine, 1971. paper.

Reviews:
    Baldwin, Barry.   Library Journal, 1 June 1970,
        p. 2179.
    Bolger, Eugenie.   "Words, Words and More Words."
        New Leader, 25 May 1970, pp. 22-24.
    Booklist, 15 June 1970, p. 1262.
    Choice, 7 (November 1970), pp. 1229-30.
    Critic, 29 (January 1971), p. 92.
    Davis, L. J.   "The Goddess Speaks with a Greek
        Accent. "   Book World, 19 April 1970, p. 3.
    Dick, Kay.   "Murdoch's Eighth. "   Spectator, 11
        September 1964, p. 346.
    Lindroth, James R.   America, 23 May 1970,
        p. 565.
    Morris, Robert K.   Saturday Review, 16 May 1970,
        p. 48.
    Murray, John J.   Best Sellers, 15 May 1970, p. 67.
    National Observer, 27 April 1970, p. 19.
    New Republic, 9 May 1970, p. 43.
    New Yorker, 13 March 1971, p. 135.
    Publishers Weekly, 30 March 1970, p. 61.
    Times (London), 13 April 1968, p. 23.
    "Unavoidable Whimsy. "   Time, 27 April 1970,
        p. 96.
    Wall, Stephen.   Listener, 10 September 1964,
        p. 401.

A14   L'HOMME DE NAZARETH

Translations:
    Belmont, Georges and Hortense Charbrier, trans.
        [French].

Reviews:
    Relations, 37 (November 1977), pp. 312-14.

See also "The Gospel According to Anthony Burgess"
[G133] and [A17].

A15   HONEY FOR THE BEARS

London: Heinemann, 1963.
New York: Norton, 1964.
London: Pan, 1965. paper.
New York: Ballantine, 1965. paper.
Harmondsworth: Penguin, 1973. paper.

Translations:
 Gotfart, Dorothea, trans. Honig für die Bären
    [German]. Tübingen: Horst Erdmann, 1967.
 _____, trans. Honig für die Bären [German].
    Reinbek bei Hamburg: Rowohlt, 1971.

Reviews:
 Adams, R. M. New York Review of Books, 23
    January 1964, p. 7.
 Amis, Kingsley. "To Russia with Torment." New
    York Times Book Review, 2 February 1964,
    p. 5.
 Books and Bookmen, 18 (September 1973), p. 138.
 Bowen, John. Punch, 3 April 1963, p. 498.
 Brooke, Jocelyn. Listener, 28 March 1963, p. 567.
 Gavin, William F. America, 8 February 1964,
    p. 200.
 "Going Red." Times Literary Supplement, 29
    March 1963, p. 213.
 Gross, John. "Everything's Here but the Kievstone
    Cops." Book Week, 9 February 1964, p. 6.
 Hamilton, A. Books and Bookmen, 10 (July 1965),
    p. 47.
 Harvey, David D. "Middle-Browed Faction."
    Southern Review, N. S. , 5 (January 1969),
    pp. 259-72.
 Hicks, Granville. "Fertile World of Anthony Bur-
    gess." Saturday Review, 15 July 1967, p. 28.
    Same as [L60].
 Hoyt, Charles Alva. "Black Market in Red Square."
    Saturday Review, 29 February 1964, pp. 33-34.
 Ivsky, Oleg. Library Journal, 1 February 1964,
    pp. 651-52.
 Lodge, David. "Picaresque and Gawky." Spectator,
    19 April 1963, p. 504.

Malin, Irving. "Sex in Print." Antioch Review,
24 (Fall 1964), pp. 408-16.
New Leader, 13 April 1964, p. 22.
New York Herald Tribune Book Review, 9 February
1964, p. 6.
New York Times Book Review, 29 February 1964,
p. 19.
Platypus, Bill. Spectator, 30 June 1973, p. 819.
Ricks, Christopher. "The Epicene." New States-
man, 5 April 1963, p. 496. Same as [L99].
"Schizoids in Leningrad." Newsweek, 3 February
1964, pp. 81-82.
Time, 24 January 1964, p. 70.
Times (London), 1 July 1973, p. 39.
Walters, Raymond, Jr. "Say It with Paperbacks."
New York Times Book Review, 4 December 1966,
p. 60.

A16 INSIDE MR. ENDERBY

London: Heinemann, 1963.
Harmondsworth: Penguin, 1966. paper.

First published under the pseudonym Joseph Kell. See
also Enderby [A10], of which this book is the second
part.

Reviews:
Books and Bookmen, 18 (September 1973), p. 138.
Brooke, Jocelyn. Listener, 25 April 1963, p. 723.
Burgess, Anthony. Yorkshire Post, 16 May 1963,
p. 4. [Burgess's review of the novel by Joseph
Kell.] Same as [G476].
Kermode, Frank. "Poetry and Borborygms."
Listener, 6 June 1968, pp. 735-36.
Observer, 27 February 1966, p. 22.
Platypus, Bill. "Paperbacks." Spectator, 30 June
1973, p. 819.
Sunday Times (London), 1 July 1973, p. 39.

A17 JESUS OF NAZARETH. By William Barclay.

Based on the film directed by Franco Zeffirelli; script
by Anthony Burgess, Suso Cecchi d'Amico, and Franco
Zeffirelli; photos by Paul Ronald.

London: Collins, 1977.
Cleveland: Collins, 1977.

See also "The Gospel According to Anthony Burgess" [G133].

A18   THE LONG DAY WANES: A MALAYAN TRILOGY

New York: Norton, 1965.
New York: Ballantine, 1966. paper.
New York: Norton, 1977. paper.

Entitled A Malayan Trilogy [A20] in England; includes Time for a Tiger [A27], The Enemy in the Blanket [A12], and Beds in the East [A03].

Reviews:
Bergonzi, Bernard. New York Review of Books, 20 May 1965, p. 15.
Best Sellers, 15 August 1966, p. 188.
Choice, 2 (September 1965), pp. 383-84.
Cruttwell, Patrick. Hudson Review, 18 (Autumn 1965), pp. 442-50.
Fleischer, L. Publishers Weekly, 4 July 1966, p. 82.
Gabriel, Brother D. Best Sellers, 1 July 1965, pp. 150-51.
Kauffmann, Stanley. "A Cycle of Cathay." New Leader, 10 May 1965, pp. 24-25.
Kirkus Service, 15 April 1965, p. 445.
New York Times Book Review, 4 September 1977, p. 23.
Ostermann, R. National Observer, 14 June 1965, p. 21.
Saturday Review, 24 September 1966, p. 40.
Time, 2 July 1965, p. 84.
Wheeler, Thomas C. "Twilight of Empire in the Malay States." New York Times Book Review, 30 May 1965, p. 14.
Woodcock, George. Pacific Affairs, 38 (Summer 1965), pp. 206-07.

A19   A LONG TRIP TO TEATIME.

New York: Stonehill, 1976. Drawings by Fulvio Testa.

Reviews:
Booklist, 1 June 1977, p. 1483.
Listener, 10 February 1977, p. 189.
New Republic, 28 May 1977, p. 41.
Times Literary Supplement, 25 March 1977, p. 348.

A20   A MALAYAN TRILOGY.

London: Heinemann, 1964.
London: Pan, 1964. paper.
Harmondsworth: Penguin, 1972. paper.

Entitled The Long Day Wanes [A18] in the U. S.;
includes Time for a Tiger [A27], The Enemy in the
Blanket [A12], and Beds in the East [A03].

Reviews:
Books and Bookmen, 17 (August 1972), p. ii.
Ratcliffe, Michael. "Fifteen Years On: A Comedy
of Babel and Misunderstanding." Times (London),
29 June 1972, p. 12.

A21   MF

London: Cape, 1971.
New York: Knopf, 1971.
New York: Ballantine, 1972. paper.
Harmondsworth: Penguin, 1973. paper.

Translations:
Cerquira, E. G., trans. Macho & Fêmea [Portuguese]
Rio de Janeiro: Artenova, 1971.

Reviews:
Adams, Phoebe. Atlantic, May 1971, p. 114.
America, 22 May 1971, p. 549.
Best Sellers, 1 May 1972, p. 71.
Booklist, 15 May 1971, p. 777.
Books and Bookmen, 16 (July 1971), p. 45.
Books and Bookmen, 18 (September 1973), p. 138.
Cheshire, David. Times (London), 17 June 1971,
p. 12.
Commentary, 52 (October 1971), p. 108.
Contemporary Review, 219 (October 1971), p. 211.
DeMott, Benjamin. "God's Plenty in a Flood of

Proper and Improper Nouns. " Saturday Review,
    27 March 1971, pp. 31, 39-41.
Donadio, Stephen. New York Times Book Review,
    4 April 1971, p. 4.
Duffey, Martha. "Algonquin Legend. " Time, 22
    March 1971, pp. 80, 82.
Encounter, 38 (June 1972), p. 57.
Guardian Weekly, 3 July 1971, p. 19.
"Higher Games. " Times Literary Supplement, 18
    June 1971, p. 693.
Horrocks, Norman. Library Journal, 15 March
    1971, p. 976.
Hudson Review, 24 (Summer 1971), p. 366.
Johnson, J. J. Survey of Contemporary Literature,
    Vol. 4, 1977, p. 4963.
Kermode, Frank. "The Algonquin Oedipus. " Lis-
    tener, 17 June 1971, pp. 790-91.
Kirkus Reviews, 1 January 1971, p. 16.
Lehmann-Haupt, Christopher. "Incest in the Widest
    Sense. " New York Times, 29 March 1971,
    p. 31.
Lindroth, James R. America, 12 June 1971, p. 616.
McInery, Ralph. Commonweal, 28 May 1971,
    pp. 290-91.
Murray, John J. Best Sellers, 1 April 1971,
    pp. 15-16.
Nash, Manning. American Journal of Sociology,
    77 (March 1972), pp. 995-96.
National Observer, 19 April 1971, p. 23.
New Leader, 19 April 1971, p. 19.
New York Times Book Review, 6 June 1971, p. 3.
New York Times Book Review, 5 December 1971,
    p. 84.
Newsweek, 19 April 1971, p. 123.
Nowell, Robert. "Words, Words, Words. " Tablet,
    3 July 1971, pp. 650-51.
Observer, 20 June 1971, p. 29.
Platypus, Bill. Spectator, 30 June 1973, p. 819.
Prairie Schooner, 46 (Spring 1972), p. 82.
Publishers Weekly, 8 February 1971, p. 78.
Punch, 30 June 1971, p. 890.
Raban, Jonathan. "Package Tour. " New Statesman,
    18 June 1971, pp. 856-57.
Sunday Times (London), 1 July 1973, p. 39.
Time, 22 March 1971, p. 80.
Waugh, Auberon. "Auberon Waugh on New Novels. "
    Spectator, 19 June 1971, pp. 849-50.

West, Paul. "A Trombone on Fire." Book World, 21 March 1971, p. 3.

Walters, Raymond, Jr. "Say It with Paperbacks." New York Times Book Review, 4 December 1966, p. 60.

A22 NAPOLEON SYMPHONY

London: Jonathan Cape, 1974.
Toronto: Clarke, Irwin, 1974.
New York: Knopf, 1974.
London: Corgi, 1976.

Translations:
Le Symphonie Napoléon [French]. Paris: Laffont, 1977.

Reviews:
Bayley, John. New York Review of Books, 19 September 1974, p. 32.
Blythe, Ronald. "Imperial Theme." Sunday Times (London), 29 September 1974, p. 39.
Book World (Washington Post), 26 May 1974, p. 1.
Book World, 8 December 1974, p. 8.
Booklist, 15 July 1974, p. 1230.
Books and Bookmen, 20 (January 1975), p. 49.
Chipchase, Paul. "Imperial Rag." Tablet, 7 December 1974, pp. 1185-86.
Commonweal, 6 December 1974, p. 239.
Economist, 30 November 1974, p. 7.
Glendinning, Victoria. New Statesman, 27 September 1974, p. 435.
Guardian Weekly, 5 October 1974, p. 19.
Halio, Jay L. "Love and the Grotesque." Southern Review, N. S. 11 (October 1975), pp. 942-48.
Kirkus Reviews, 15 March 1974, p. 318.
Lennon, Peter. Sunday Times (London), 1 December 1974, p. 39.
Listener, 24 October 1974, p. 552.
McKenzie, Robb. Library Journal, 15 May 1974, p. 1406.
Morris, R. K. Nation, 3 August 1974, p. 87.
Murray, John J. Best Sellers, 1 July 1974, pp. 154-55.
National Observer, 15 June 1974, p. 21.
New York Times Book Review, 1 December 1974, p. 70.

New Yorker, 8 July 1974, p. 80.
Newsweek, 27 May 1974, p. 85.
Nordell, Roderick. Christian Science Monitor, 29
    May 1974, p. 5.
Observer, 29 September 1974, p. 31.
O'Hara, J. D. New Republic, 31 August 1974,
    p. 32.
Platypus, Bill. Spectator, 28 September 1974,
    p. 405.
Publishers Weekly, 25 March 1974, p. 50.
Publishers Weekly, 13 October 1975, p. 113.
Queen's Quarterly, 82 (Summer 1975), pp. 292-94.
Raban, Jonathan. "What Shall We Do About Anthony
    Burgess?" Encounter, 43 (November 1974),
    pp. 83-88. Same as [L97].
Ratcliffe, Michael. "Set to Beethoven." Times
    (London), 26 September 1974, p. 10.
Sale, Roger. "Fooling Around, and Serious Busi-
    ness." Hudson Review, 27 (Winter 1974-1975),
    pp. 623-35.
Sanborn, Sara. New York Times Book Review, 9
    June 1974, p. 5.
Sheppard, R. Z. Time, 27 May 1974, p. 92.
Times (London), 16 May 1976, p. 39.
Times Literary Supplement, 27 September 1974,
    p. 1033.
Trewin, Ian. Times (London), 1 May 1976, p. 11.
Village Voice, 4 July 1974, p. 19.

A23   1985

Boston: Little, Brown, 1978.
London: Hutchinson, 1978.

Reviews:
    Amis, Martin. "A Stoked-Up 1976." New York
        Times Book Review, 19 November 1978, pp. 3,
        60, 62.
    Booklist, 15 September 1978, p. 146.
    Critic, 2 January 1979, p. 2.
    Economist, 14 October 1978, p. 144.
    Elledge, Jim. Library Journal, 15 September 1978,
        p. 1765.
    Fraser, G. S. "Anthony Longmug?" Listener,
        19 October 1978, pp. 517-18.
    Granetz, Marc. New Republic, 18 November 1978,
        p. 38.

Guardian Weekly, 15 October 1978, p. 21.
Human Events, 14 October 1978, p. 7.
Irwin, Michael. "Tucland, their Tucland." Times
   Literary Supplement, 6 October 1978, p. 1109.
Jamal, Zahir. New Statesman, 6 October 1978,
   p. 444.
James, Clive. New York Review of Books, 23
   November 1978, p. 16.
Kirkus Reviews, 1 August 1978, p. 822.
Lacy, Allen. "Burgess's '1985': 7 Years to Caca-
   topia." Chronicle of Higher Education, 11 De-
   cember 1978, Review Section, p. 13.
Maclean's, 6 November 1978, p. 61.
McLellan, Joseph. "O Brave New Worlds." Book
   World (Washington Post), 12 November 1978,
   p. 5.
New Leader, 20 November 1978, p. 16.
Nordell, Roderick. "Beyond '1984' But Not Up to
   It." Christian Science Monitor, 13 (November
   1978), Section B, p. 15.
Observer (London), 1 October 1978, p. 34.
Prescott, Peter S. Newsweek, 9 October 1978,
   p. 105.
Publishers Weekly, 18 September 1978, p. 161.
Revzin, Philip. "'Tukland': Grim Alternate to
   Orwell's Future." Wall Street Journal, 21
   November 1978, p. 24.

A24   NOTHING LIKE THE SUN: A STORY OF SHAKE-
      SPEARE'S LOVE-LIFE

London: Heinemann, 1964.
New York: Norton, 1964.
Don Mills, Ontario: Collins, 1964.
New York: Ballantine, 1965. paper.
Harmondsworth: Penguin, 1966. paper.
New York: Norton, 1975. paper.

Translations:
   Oilmarks, Ake, trans. Intet Är Som Solen: En
      Berättelse om Shakespeares Käreksliv [Swedish].
      Stockholm: Bonnier, 1964.

Reviews:
   Buitenhuis, Peter. "A Lusty Man Was Will." New
      York Times Book Review, 13 September 1964,
      pp. 5, 26.

Choice, 1 (January 1965), p. 477.

Enright, D. J. "Mr. W. S." New Statesman, 24
April 1964, pp. 642-44. Same as [J10].

Garrett, George. Survey of Contemporary Literature, Vol. 8, 1977, p. 5431.

Halio, Jay L. "A Sense of the Present." Southern
Review, N. S. 2 (October 1966), pp. 953-66.

"Jakes Peer or Jacques Père." Times Literary
Supplement, 23 April 1964, p. 329.

Jennings, Elizabeth. Listener, 23 April 1964,
p. 693.

Kauffmann, Stanley. "Filling in the Blank Verses
of a Man on the Make." Book Week, 20 September 1964, p. 5.

Lamott, Kenneth. "Burgess and Bellow." Show,
4, No. 11 (December 1964), p. 80.

McCabe, Bernard. "No Bardolatry." Commonweal,
30 October 1964, pp. 174-75.

Masterplots Annual, 1965, p. 215.

Miller, Warren. "Enter Will, Dressed in Prose."
Nation, 5 October 1964, pp. 196-97.

New York Herald Tribune Book Review, 20 September 1964, p. 5.

Observer, 11 September 1966, p. 22.

Pippett, Aileen. "The Sonneteer Was Not All Talk."
Saturday Review, 17 October 1964, p. 38.

Raymond, J. Punch, 10 August 1966, p. 233.

Ryan, Stephen P. Best Sellers, 1 October 1964,
pp. 259-60.

Sale, Roger. "Provincial Champions and Grandmasters." Hudson Review, 17 (Winter 1964-
1965), pp. 608-18.

Time, 8 January 1965, p. 71.

Vansittart, Peter. "Primary Colours." Spectator,
24 April 1964, p. 561.

A25   ONE HAND CLAPPING

London: Peter Davies, 1961.
London: Transworld, 1963. [Corgi.]
New York: Knopf, 1972.
New York: Ballantine, 1973. paper.
London: Peter Davies, 1974.

First published under the pseudonym Joseph Kell.

Translations:
Lundgren, Caj, trans. Applåd med en Hand [Swed-
ish]. Stockholm: Wahlström and Widstrand,
1973.

Reviews:
Adams, Phoebe. Atlantic, March 1972, p. 108.
Booklist, 1 May 1972, p. 752.
Brickner, R. P. New York Times Book Review,
12 March 1972, p. 4.
Choice, 9 (November 1972), p. 1126.
Cooper, Arthur. Newsweek, 6 March 1972, p. 78.
Foote, Audrey. Book World, 5 March 1972, p. 7.
Hudson Review, 25 (Summer 1972), p. 330.
Kirkus Reviews, 1 December 1971, p. 1272.
Moore, H. T. Saturday Review, 12 February 1972,
p. 73.
Murray, John J. Best Sellers, 15 February 1972,
p. 514.
New York Times Book Review, 4 June 1972, p. 24.
New York Times Book Review, 3 December 1972,
p. 78.
Publishers Weekly, 29 November 1971, p. 31.
Publishers Weekly, 8 January 1973, p. 66.
Sayre, Ed. Library Journal, 15 February 1972,
p. 698.
Sheppard, R. Z. "Clockwork Kumquat." Time,
14 February 1972, pp. 73-74.
Wilson, Edmund. New Yorker, 18 March 1972,
pp. 153-56.
"Winners Weepers." Christian Science Monitor,
10 February 1972, p. 10.

A26   THE RIGHT TO AN ANSWER

London: Heinemann, 1960.
New York: Norton, 1961.
New York: Ballantine, 1966. paper.
London: New English Library, 1968.
New York: Norton, 1978. paper.

Reviews:
Bliven, Naomi. "Ordeals and Orgies." New
Yorker, 8 April 1961, pp. 169-74.
Booklist, 15 January 1961, p. 292.
Coleman, John. "Music Week." Spectator, 27

May 1960, p. 778.
Fink, John. Chicago Sunday Tribune, 8 January
    1961, p. 4.
Kennedy, A. R. Library Journal, 15 December
    1960, pp. 4485-86.
Kirkus Service, 1 November 1960, p. 937.
Laski, Marghanita. "Morality with Heart." Satur-
    day Review, 28 January 1961, p. 17.
"Local Boys Make Good." Times Literary Supple-
    ment, 3 June 1960, p. 349.
Nordell, Rod. "The Comedy of Discontent." Chris-
    tian Science Monitor, 19 January 1961, p. 5.
Petersen, C. Books Today (Chicago Sunday Trib-
    une), 29 May 1966, p. 9.
Price, R. G. G. Punch, 25 May 1960, p. 739.
Raymond, John. Listener, 23 June 1960, p. 1111.
Shrapnel, Norman. Guardian, 27 May 1960, p. 9.
Springfield Republican, 29 January 1961, Sec. D,
    p. 4.
Talbot, Daniel. "A Wry and Comic Novel." Lively
    Arts and Book Review, 22 January 1961, p. 32.
Time, 20 January 1961, p. 91.
Times (London), 24 February 1968, p. 20.
Walters, Raymond, Jr. "Say It with Paperbacks."
    New York Times Book Review, 4 December
    1966, p. 60.
Williams, David. "On Leave and On the Job."
    Time and Tide, 11 June 1960, p. 679.
_____. Times Literary Supplement, 3 June
    1960, p. 349.

A27   TIME FOR A TIGER

London: Heinemann, 1956.
London: Heinemann, 1964.   Reprint.
London: Heinemann, 1968.   Reissue.

Included as part of A Malayan Trilogy [A20] and The
Long Day Wanes [A18].

A28   TREMOR OF INTENT: AN ESCHATOLOGICAL SPY
       NOVEL

London: Heinemann, 1966.
New York: Norton, 1966.

Harmondsworth: Penguin, 1969. paper.
New York: Ballantine, 1972. paper.
New York: Norton, 1977. paper.

Translations:
> Arthens, Edith, trans. A última missão [Portuguese]. Rio de Janeiro: Artenova, 1973.
> Canto, Patricio, trans. Trémula Intención [Spanish]. Buenos Aires: Sudamericana, 1972.
> Deutsch, Michel, trans. Un agent qui vous veut du bien [French]. Paris: Denoël, 1969.
> _____, trans. Un agent qui vous veut du bien [French]. Paris: Gallimard, 1973.
> Lundgren, Caj, trans. Skuggen ar ett Svek [Swedish]. Stockholm: Wahlström and Widstrand, 1972.
> Mortensen, Harry, trans. Martyrernes Blod [Danish]. Copenhagen: Spektrum, 1969.

Reviews:
> America, 26 November 1966, p. 708.
> Best Sellers, 1 September 1972, p. 262.
> Bliven, N. New Yorker, 11 February 1967, p. 159.
> Choice, 4 (July-August 1967), p. 530.
> Cook, Bruce. "Spying, the Cold War and Eschatology." National Catholic Reporter, 18 January 1967, p. 9.
> Crinklaw, Don. Commonweal, 16 December 1966, pp. 329-30.
> Cromie, A. Books Today (Chicago Sunday Tribune), 13 November 1966, p. 17.
> Daniel, John. "Who's Your Agent?" Spectator, 10 June 1966, pp. 733-34.
> Davis, Robert Gorham. "Invaded Selves." Hudson Review, 19 (Winter 1966-1967), pp. 659-68.
> Dolbier, M. World Journal Tribune, 7 October 1966, p. 20.
> Dollen, Charles. Best Sellers, 15 October 1966, p. 254.
> Duchene, A. Manchester Guardian Weekly, 16 June 1966, p. 11.
> Evans, Fallon. "The Ultimate Spy." Critic, 25, No. 4 (February-March 1967), pp. 78-79.
> Gardner, John. "More Smog from the Dark Satanic Mills." Southern Review, N. S. 5 (January 1969), pp. 224-44.
> Graver, Lawrence. "House of Burgesses." New

Republic, 15 October 1966, pp. 25, 27.
Harris, L. Punch, 22 June 1966, p. 926.
Hatch, Robert. "A Tour of the Pops." Nation,
 5 December 1966, pp. 620-21.
Kirkus Service, 15 September 1966, p. 1007.
Kitching, J. Publishers Weekly, 26 September
 1966, p. 131.
Lejeune, Anthony. "Bond in Greenland." Tablet,
 30 July 1966, p. 872.
Levitas, G. Book World, 12 November 1967, p. 23.
Lindroth, James R. America, 22 October 1966,
 p. 492.
Lord, J. Life, 14 October 1966, p. 10.
Maloff, Saul. "Sin Was a Chronic Disease." Sat-
 urday Review, 29 October 1966, pp. 32-33.
Mayne, Richard. New Statesman, 10 June 1966,
 p. 852.
_____. "Spy in the Sky." Spectator, 10 June
 1966, p. 733.
Month, 36 (September 1966), p. 154.
Moon, Eric. "Joyous Cynicism." Book Week, 9
 October 1966, p. 2.
New York Times Book Review, 24 April 1877, p. 49.
Ostermann, R. National Observer, 31 October 1966,
 p. 20.
Pritchard, William H. "The Burgess Memorandum."
 Partisan Review, 34 (1967), pp. 319-23.
Publishers Weekly, 11 September 1967, p. 71.
Ready, William. Library Journal, November 1966,
 p. 5426.
Richardson, M. Observer, 5 June 1966, p. 26.
Saturday Review, 25 October 1969, p. 42.
Schott, Webster. "A New Order of Things." New
 York Times Book Review, 16 October 1966,
 p. 4.
Time, 14 October 1966, p. 125.
Times Literary Supplement, 9 June 1966, p. 509.
Tisdall, J. Books and Bookmen, 11 (August 1966),
 p. 34.
Tucker, Martin. Commonweal, 2 December 1966,
 pp. 273-74.
Virginia Quarterly Review, 43 (Winter 1967),
 p. x.
Willett, John. "Burgess's New Novel." Listener,
 9 June 1966, p. 849.

A29   A VISION OF BATTLEMENTS

London: Sidgwick and Jackson, 1965. Illus. by
    Edward Pagram.
New York: Norton, 1966.
New York: Ballantine, 1966. paper.

Reviews:
    Baumbach, Elinor. "Stranded on Gibraltar." Sat-
        urday Review, 29 January 1966, p. 38.
    Brooke, Jocelyn. Listener, 30 September 1965,
        p. 505.
    Choice, 3 (July-August 1966), p. 408.
    Coleman, J. Observer, 26 September 1965, p. 28.
    "The Ennead." Times Literary Supplement, 30
        September 1965, p. 850.
    Gardner, John. Southern Review, N.S. 3 (April
        1967), p. 444.
    Hackett, A. Publishers Weekly, 10 October 1966,
        p. 75.
    Hoyt, Charles Alva. Commonweal, 25 March 1966,
        pp. 33-35.
    Knickerbocker, Conrad. "Variations on an Anti-
        heroic Theme." New York Times, 1 February
        1966, p. 33.
    New Yorker, 7 May 1966, p. 186.
    Newsweek, 21 February 1966, p. 104.
    Ostermann, R. National Observer, 9 May 1966,
        p. 25.
    Ricks, Christopher. "Rude Forerunner." New
        Statesman, 24 September 1965, pp. 444-45.
    Saturday Review, 26 November 1966, p. 40.
    Shuttleworth, M. Punch, 20 October 1965, p. 588.
    Swanson, Stanley. Library Journal, 1 April 1966,
        pp. 1920-21.
    Time, 4 February 1966, p. 107.
    Vansittart, Peter. Spectator, 1 October 1965,
        pp. 424-25.
    Wheeler, Thomas C. New York Times Book Review,
        30 January 1966, p. 32.
    Wood, Frederick T. "Current Literature 1965: I.
        Poetry, Prose and Drama." English Studies,
        47 (August 1966), pp. 314-25.

A30   THE WANTING SEED

London: Heinemann, 1962.

New York: Ballantine, 1962. paper.
New York: Norton, 1963.
New York: Ballantine, 1964. paper.
London: Pan, 1965. paper.
New York: Ballantine, 1970. paper.
Harmondsworth: Penguin, 1973. paper.
New York: Norton, 1976. paper.

Translations:
Belmont, Georges, and Hortense Chabrier, trans.
La Folle semence [French]. Paris: Laffont,
1973.
Kazue, Saitô and Kuroyanagi Hisaya, trans. Miko-
mo No Nai Shushi [Japanese]. Tokyo: Hayakawa
Shobô, 1973.
Tjen, Michael, trans. Du Skal Aede din Naeste
[Danish]. Copenhagen: Schonborg, 1963.

Reviews:
Books and Bookmen, 18 (September 1973), p. 138.
Brophy, Brigid. "Not Very Brave, Not So New."
Book Week, 3 November 1963, pp. 6, 25.
Buitenhuis, Peter. "A Battle Between the Sexes
Was the Answer." New York Times Book Re-
view, 27 October 1963, pp. 4, 20.
Canton, Robert F. Library Journal, 1 October
1963, p. 3641.
Dempsey, David. "Fi, Fi, Fo, Fum ...." Satur-
day Review, 23 November 1963, pp. 43-44.
Hamilton, A. Books and Bookmen, 10 (July 1965),
47.
"The Hungry Sheep." Times Literary Supplement,
5 October 1962, p. 773.
Keown, Eric. Punch, 17 October 1962, pp. 575-76.
Maguire, Clinton J. Best Sellers, 1 November
1963, p. 277.
New Yorker, 2 November 1963, pp. 209-10.
Platypus, Bill. Spectator, 30 June 1973, p. 819.
Sunday Times (London), 1 July 1973, p. 39.
Taubman, Robert. "Prospects." New Statesman,
5 October 1962, pp. 460-61.
Time, 6 December 1963, p. 123.
Times Literary Supplement, 5 October 1962, p. 773.
Walters, Raymond, J. "Say It with Paperbacks."
New York Times Book Review, 4 December 1966,
p. 60.
Wilkie, Brian. "Satiric Ramble." Commonweal,

17 January 1964, p. 465.
"World Without Sex." <u>Newsweek</u>, 28 October 1963,
pp. 101-02.

A31 THE WORM AND THE RING

London: Heinemann, 1961.
London: Heinemann, 1970. Revised edition.

<u>Reviews:</u>
Price, R. G. G. <u>Punch</u>, 28 June 1961, pp. 989-90.
Raven, Simon. "<u>Verdicts</u> of Guilty." <u>Spectator</u>,
2 June 1961, p. 808.
"Sparing the Rod." <u>Times Literary Supplement</u>,
7 July 1961, p. 421.

B. STORIES

B01 "An American Organ." Mad River Review, 1 (Winter 1964-1965), pp. 33-39.

B02 "A Benignant Growth." Transatlantic Review, No. 32 (Summer 1969), pp. 10-15.

B03 "From It Is the Miller's Daughter: A Novel in Progress." Transatlantic Review, No. 24 (Spring 1967), pp. 5-15.

B04 "Gibraltar." In Integrated Writing. By R. C. K. Ginn. Beverly Hills, Calif.: Glenco Press, 1970.

B05 "The Muse: A Sort of SF Story." Hudson Review, 21 (Spring 1968), pp. 109-26.

B06 "Somebody's Got to Pay the Rent." Partisan Review, 35 (Winter 1968), pp. 67-74.

C. POEMS

C01 "Five Revolutionary Sonnets: From the Novels Inside Mr. Enderby and Enderby Outside." Transatlantic Review, No. 21 (Summer 1966), pp. 30-32.

C02 "Imagination Is Your True Apollo." New York Times, 12 July 1969, p. 17.

C03 MOSES: A NARRATIVE

London: Dempsey and Squires, 1976.
New York: Stonehill, 1976.

Reviews:
Daiches, David. Times Literary Supplement, 21 January 1977, p. 50.
Fletcher, C. Booklist, 15 October 1976, p. 300.
Listener, 10 February 1977, p. 189.
Publishers Weekly, 28 June 1976, p. 91.
Saturday Review, 24 July 1976, p. 27.
Soete, Mary. Library Journal, 1 December 1976, p. 2494.
Solomon, Albert J. Best Sellers, 36 (November 1976), p. 264.
Village Voice, 29 March 1976, p. 42.
Wood, Michael, New York Times Review of Books, 30 September 1976, pp. 40-42.

C04 "O Lord, O Ford, God Help Us, Also You." New York Times Magazine, 29 December 1974, pp. 6-7.

C05 "On Christ's Nativity: Five Sonnets." Times Literary Supplement, 23 January 1976, p. 76.

C06 "The Sword." Transatlantic Review, No. 23 (Winter 1966-1967), pp. 41-43.

D. NON-FICTION BOOKS, SECTIONS OF BOOKS
(with translations and reviews)

D01 "The Case for Diversity." In New Movements in the
Study and Teaching of English. Ed. Nicholas Bagnell. London: Temple Smith, 1973, pp. 115-24.

D02 ENGLISH LITERATURE: A SURVEY FOR STUDENTS

London: Longmans, Green, 1958.
London: Longmans, 1966.
London: Longmans, 1974. New edition. paper.

Translations:
English Literature [French]. Paris: Colin, 1974.
Fukuda, Rikutaro and Hisashi Shigeo, trans.
Igirisu Bungakushi [Japanese]. Tokyo: Dabiddo-
sha, 1959.

First published under the name John Burgess Wilson.

D03 ERNEST HEMINGWAY AND HIS WORLD

London: Thames and Hudson, 1978.
New York: Scribner's, 1978.

Reviews:
Adams, P. -L. Atlantic, October 1978, p. 116.
America, 2 December 1978, p. 414.
Beatty, Jack. New Republic, 7 October 1978,
pp. 37-38.
Best Sellers, February 1979, p. 363.
Booklist, 15 September 1978, p. 146.
Critic, 15 November 1978, p. 7.
Cross, Jack. "For Him the Bell Tolls." Times

33

Educational Supplement, 20 October 1978, p. 24.
Horn Book Magazine, December 1978, p. 669.
Kirkus Reviews, 1 July 1978, p. 723.
New Statesman, 27 October 1978, p. 549.
Ott, William. Library Journal, August 1978,
   p. 1510.
Publishers Weekly, 24 July 1978, p. 92.
Shone, Richard. "Crack-up." Spectator, 25
   November 1978, p. 23.

D04   "Foreword." Anthony Burgess: A Bibliography:
       Works By and About Him Complete with Selected
       Annotations. 2nd ed. By Paul W. Boytinck. [?]:
       Norwood Editions, 1977.

D05   "Genesis and Headache." In Afterwords: Novelists
       on Their Novels. Ed. Thomas McCormack. New
       York: Harper, 1969, pp. 28-47.

       Discusses the writing of Nothing Like the Sun [A24].

D06   [Untitled Chapter]. In The God I Want. Ed. James
       Mitchell. London: Constable, 1967, pp. 57-70.
       Indianapolis: Bobbs-Merrill, 1967, pp. 57-70.

D07   HERE COMES EVERYBODY: AN INTRODUCTION TO
       JAMES JOYCE FOR THE ORDINARY READER

       London: Faber and Faber, 1965.
       London: Faber, 1969. paper.

       Entitled Re Joyce [D24] in the U.S.

       Translations:
           Triesch, Gisela and Manfred Triesch, trans. Ein
           Mann in Dublin Namens Joyce [German]. Bad
           Homburg: Gehlen, 1968.

       Reviews:
           Donoghue, Denis. "Wortsampler." New Statesman,
           17 September 1965, p. 402.
           "Finnagain." Economist, 4 December 1965, p. 1095.
           Furbank, P. N. Manchester Guardian Weekly, 23
           September 1965, p. 10.

Hart, Clive. Modern Language Review, 62 (October 1967) pp. 714-15.

Hodgart, Matthew. "Haveth Critics Everywhere." Encounter, 25 (November 1965), pp. 78, 82.

Hollis, Christopher. "James Joyce." Tablet, 6 November 1965, p. 1241.

"Joyce's Burgessbook." Times Literary Supplement, 4 November 1965, p. 972.

Rodgers, W. R. Listener, 11 November 1965, p. 767.

Seymour-Smith, Martin. "Joyce the Great." Spectator, 24 September 1965, p. 384.

Toynbee, P. Observer, 3 October 1965, p. 26.

D08   "Introduction." All About H. Hatterr. By G[ovindas] V[ishnaodas] Desani. New York: Farrar, Straus and Giroux, 1970, pp. 7-11.

D09   "Introduction." Augustus Carp, Esq. by Himself: Being the Autobiography of a Really Good Man. By Henry Howarth Bashford. London: Heinemann, 1966, pp. xii-xiv.

Reviews:
Times Literary Supplement, 6 October 1966, p. 913.

Excerpt reprinted as "Augustus Carp Addresses a New Generation of Sinners" [G30].

D10   "Introduction." Don Giovanni and Idomeneo. By W. A. Mozart. London: Cassell, 1971, pp. 7-22. Cassell Opera Guides. New York: Universe Books, 1971.

D11   "Introduction." The John Collier Reader. By John Collier. New York: Knopf, 1972, xi-xv.

Reviews:
Financial Post, 5 May 1973, p. 67.
Lash, Thomas. "Chimps, Manikins, People Too." New York Times, 25 November 1972, Sect. L, p. 29.

D12 "Introduction." Last Exit to Brooklyn. By Hubert
Selby, Jr. London: Calder and Boyars, 1968.
2nd ed. London: Calder and Boyars, 1970. [Dis-
tributed by Corgi.]

D13 "Introduction." Titus Groan. By Mervyn Peake.
London: Eyre and Spottiswoode, 1968, pp. 9-13.

D14 "Introduction." The White Company. By Arthur
Conan Doyle. London: Murray, 1975.

D15 "Is America Falling Apart?" In The Norton Reader:
An Anthology of Expository Prose. 3rd ed. Arthur
M. Eastman, General Editor; Caesar Blake, Hubert
M. English, Jr., Alan B. Howes, Robert T.
Lenaghan, Leo F. McNamara, James Rosier, Edi-
tors. New York: Norton, 1973, pp. 424-29.

Reprint of Burgess's article [G178].

D16 JOYSPRICK: AN INTRODUCTION TO THE LANGUAGE
OF JAMES JOYCE

London: Deutsch, 1973. The Language Library.
New York: Academic Press, 1973.
New York: Harcourt Brace Jovanovich, 1975. paper.

Reviews:
Book World, 29 June 1975, p. 4.
Books and Bookmen, 18 (September 1973), p. 60.
Eckley, Grace. "James Joyce." Contemporary
Literature, 16 (Autumn 1975), pp. 504-15.
Fox, Jay. Modern Fiction Studies. 21 (Summer
1975), pp. 264-67.
Goldman, Arnold. Review of English Studies, N.S.
25 (November 1974), pp. 495-98.
Guardian Weekly, 23 June 1973, p. 26.
Luckett, Richard. "Richard Luckett on Joyce,
Beckett and the Word." Spectator, 30 June 1973,
p. 815-16.
Observer, 24 June 1973, p. 32.
Sunday Times, 24 June 1973, p. 38.
Times Higher Education Supplement, 10 August
1973, p. 12.

Times Literary Supplement, 15 June 1973, p. 699.

D17 LANGUAGE MADE PLAIN

London: English Universities Press, 1964.
New York: Crowell, 1965.
New York: Crowell, 1969.
New York: Apollo Editions, 1969. paper.

First published under the name John Burgess Wilson.

Reviews:
Adams, J. Donald. "A Common Heritage." New
    York Times Book Review, 28 March 1965, p. 26.
Books and Bookmen, 21 (February 1976), p. 20.
Choice, 2 (October 1965), p. 480.
Close, R. A. Modern Language Review, 60
    (January 1965), pp. 84-85.
Cook, Margaret C. "Language." Library Journal,
    1 June 1965, p. 2554.
Dolbier, M. New York Herald Tribune, 8 February
    1965, p. 123.
Gosling, Ray. Times (London), 3 April 1976, p. 11.
Harrison, Joseph G. "From the Bookshelf."
    Christian Science Monitor, 1 March 1965, p. 13.
"Preaching Polyglottism." Times Literary Supple-
    ment, 23 April 1964, p. 337.
Publishers Weekly, 4 August 1969, p. 50.
Quarterly Journal of Speech, 57 (February 1971),
    p. 123.

D18 NEW YORK

Amsterdam: Time-Life, 1976. Photos by Dan Budnik
    et al.
New York: Time-Life, 1977. Great Cities Series.

Reviews:
Fisher, Antonia. "Tale of Two Cities." Sunday
    Times (London), 15 May 1977, p. 41.
Loprete, N. J., Jr. Best Sellers, 37 (July 1977),
    p. 115.
Publishers Weekly, 28 February 1977, p. 115.
Rickleft, R. Wall Street Journal, 6 June 1977,
    p. 16.

Walters, R. New York Times Book Review, 6 March 1977, pp. 32-33.

D19 THE NOVEL NOW: A GUIDE TO CONTEMPORARY FICTION

New York: Norton, 1967.
New York: Pegasus, 1970. paper.
London: Faber, 1971. Revised edition.

Entitled The Novel Now: A Student's Guide to Contemporary Literature in England [D20].

Translations:
Yuichi, Makawa, trans. Gendai Shosetsu To Wa Nanika [Japanese]. Tokyo: Takeuchi Shoten, 1970.

Reviews:
Bergonzi, Bernard. Hudson Review, 21 (Summer 1968), p. 355.
Booklist, 15 January 1968, p. 580.
Books and Bookmen, 17 (April 1972), p. 61.
Hicks, Granville. "The Novel Today and Tomorrow." Saturday Review, 25 November 1967, pp. 33-34.
Hoggart, R. Manchester Guardian Weekly, 13 July 1967, p. 11.
Kirkus Service, 1 October 1967, p. 1236.
Lodge, David. Spectator, 18 August 1967, p. 190.
New York Times Book Review, 7 January 1968, p. 18.
Newlove, Donald. "The Contemporary Novel Through the Eyes of a Pro." Book World, 3 December 1967, p. 32.
Observer, 20 August 1967, p. 18.
Pritchard, William H. "Burgess vs. Scholes." Novel, 2 (1969), pp. 164-67.
Publishers Weekly, 20 November 1967, p. 55.
Sale, Roger. "Nothing Like the English." Massachusetts Review, 9 (Winter 1968), pp. 181-84.
Simms, Theodore F. Library Journal, 15 October 1967, p. 3642.
Times Literary Supplement, 27 June 1968, p. 680.
Times Literary Supplement, 21 April 1972, p. 439.
Vonalt, Larry P. "Of Time and Literature." Sewanee Review, 77 (Winter 1969), pp. 164-70.

D20 THE NOVEL NOW: A STUDENT'S GUIDE TO CON-
TEMPORARY LITERATURE

London: Faber, 1967.
London: Faber, 1971. New edition.

Entitled The Novel Now: A Guide to Contemporary
Fiction in the U.S. [D19].

Reviews:
Bergonzi, Bernard. "Fiction and Fabulation."
Hudson Review, 21 (Summer 1968), pp. 355-64.
Grigson, Geoffrey. "Insatiable Liking." Listener,
7 November 1968, pp. 618-19. Same as [J12].
Lodge, David. "House of Fiction." Spectator, 18
August 1967, p. 190.
Murray, Patrick. Studies, 62 (Spring 1973),
pp. 98-100.

D21 THE NOVEL TO-DAY

London: Longmans, for the British Council and the
National Book League, 1963. Writers and Their
Work Series.
London: Longmans, 1967. American edition.
London: Longmans, for the British Council and the
National Book League, 1971. Reprint.
[London?]: Folcroft Library Editions, 1971.

Review:
Ricks, Christopher. "The Epicene." New Statesman, 5 April 1963, p. 496. Same as [L99].

D22 OBSCENITY AND THE ARTS

Valletta: Malta Library Association, 1973.

D23 "The Politics of Graham Greene." In Page 2: The
Best of "Speaking of Books" from the New York
Times Book Review. Ed. Francis Brown. New
York: Holt, Rinehart and Winston, 1969, pp. 284-
91.

Same as [G323].

D24   REJOYCE

New York: Norton, 1965.
New York: Ballantine, 1965. paper.
New York: Norton, 1968. paper.
New York: Peter Smith, 1968.

Entitled Here Comes Everybody [D07] in England

Reviews:
Booklist, 15 December 1965, p. 393.
Choice, 3 (July-August 1966), p. 408.
Donoghue, Denis. New Statesman, 17 September
  1965, p. 402.
Dublin Magazine, 5, No. 1 (Spring 1966), p. 85.
Economist, 4 December 1965, p. 1095.
English, 16 (Autumn 1966), p. 111.
Fremont-Smith, E. New York Times, 1 December
  1965, p. 49.
Hackett, A. Publishers Weekly, 10 October 1966,
  p. 75.
Hatch, Robert. "His Fame Proceeds in Giant
  Steps." Harper's, March 1966, pp. 142-43, 146.
Hodgart, Matthew. Encounter, 25 (November 1965),
  p. 78.
Kain, R. M. Criticism, 9 (Winter 1967), p. 102.
Kirkus Service, 15 October 1965, p. 1106.
Lewald, H. E. Carleton Miscellany, 7 (Spring
  1966), pp. 124-25.
New Yorker, 15 January 1966, p. 120.
Noon, William T. James Joyce Quarterly, 3
  (Spring 1966), pp. 215-19.
O'Dea, Richard J. "Joyce Tri-umphant." Southern
  Review, N. S. , 4 (January 1968), pp. 259-63.
Poirer, Richard. "No Invitation to Tea." New
  York Times Book Review, 9 January 1966, p. 6.
Porter, Raymond. Catholic World, 203 (April
  1966), pp. 61-62.
Publishers Weekly, 25 December 1967, p. 63.
Sears, W. P. Education, 87 (September 1966),
  p. 61.
Sewanee Review, 77 (July 1969), p. 543.
Staley, Thomas F. Commonweal, 4 March 1966,
  pp. 645-46.
Sullivan, A. M. "The Sanctification of the Ordi-
  nary." Saturday Review, 25 December 1965,
  pp. 34-35.

D25 "The Seventeenth Novel." In Page 2: The Best of "Speaking of Books" from the New York Times Book Review. Ed. Francis Brown. New York: Holt, Rinehart and Winston, 1969, pp. 85-89. Reprint of [G363].

D26 SHAKESPEARE

London: Jonathan Cape, 1970.
New York: Knopf, 1970.
Harmondsworth: Penguin, 1972. paper.

Translations:
Paris: Buchet-Chastel, 1977 [French].
Sissung, Maud, and Bernard Noël, trans. Paris: Buchet/Chastel, 1972 [French].

Reviews:
Adams, Phoebe. Atlantic, September 1970, p. 143.
Best Sellers, 15 November 1970, p. 357.
Book World, 1 May 1977, Sec. E, p. 7.
Booklist, 15 February 1971, p. 470.
Books and Bookmen, 16 (November 1970), p. 40.
Books and Bookmen, 18 (January 1973), p. 124.
Brown, Ivor. "Shakespeare Panorama." Drama, No. 99 (Winter 1970), pp. 63-64.
Butler, Francelia. Library Journal, 15 November 1970, p. 3909.
Contemporary Review, 218 (March 1971), p. 168.
DeMott, Benjamin. "Will the Real Shakespeare Please Stand Up?" Saturday Review, 7 November 1970, pp. 31-32, 35, 46-47.
Eagleton, Terry. Commonweal, 30 October 1970, pp. 129-31.
Kirkus Reviews, 1 September 1970, p. 1024.
Kliatt Paperback Book Guide, 11 (Spring 1977), p. 20.
Lask, Thomas. "The Making of a Monument." New York Times, 24 December 1970, p. 19.
Lewis, Naomi. "Shakespeare and the Readers." New Statesman, 25 December 1970, pp. 870-71.
Lucy, Sean. "William the Silent." Tablet, 6 February 1971, p. 135.
National Review, 15 December 1970, p. 1358.
New York Times Book Review, 24 December 1970, p. 19.

"A Novel Picture." Economist, 17 October 1970,
pp. 60-61.
Potter, Dennis. Times (London), 24 September
1970, p. 15.
Publishers Weekly, 5 October 1970, p. 62.
"Shakespeare: The Works and the Worker." Times
Literary Supplement, 11 December 1970, p. 1440.
Virginia Quarterly Review, 47 (Spring 1971),
pp. lxvii, lxx.
Wall Street Journal, 20 January 1971, p. 14.
Yale Review, 60 (March 1971), p. 456.

D27   URGENT COPY: LITERARY STUDIES

London: Jonathan Cape, 1968.
New York: Norton, 1968.
Harmondsworth: Penguin, 1973. paper.

Reviews:
"Beyond the Pleasure Principle." Times Literary
Supplement, 13 March 1969, pp. 259-60.
Booklist, 1 June 1969, p. 1107.
Books and Bookmen, 18 (September 1973), p. 138.
Browne, Joseph. America, 29 March 1969,
pp. 369-70.
Choice, 6 (January 1970), p. 91.
Cutler, Edward J. Library Journal, 15 (March
1969), p. 1147.
Dick, Susan. Queen's Quarterly, 76 (Summer 1969),
pp. 306-07.
Doyle, Paul A. Best Sellers, 1 April 1969, pp. 3-
4.
Feeney, William J. "Some Elegant Essays."
Catholic World, 209 (July 1969), pp. 190-91.
Grigson, Geoffrey. "Insatiable Liking." Listener,
7 November 1968, p. 618. Same as [J12].
Kirkus Reviews, 1 January 1969, p. 36.
Library Journal, 15 March 1969, p. 1147.
London Magazine, 8 (November 1968), pp. 110-112.
Macauley, Robie. New York Times Book Review,
30 March 1969, p. 4.
Mitchell, Julian. "High Hack." New Statesman,
15 November 1968, p. 678.
New York Times, 20 March 1969, p. 45.
Progressive, 33, No. 5 (May 1969), p. 48.
Publishers Weekly, 20 January 1969, p. 264.

Spectator, 30 June 1973, p. 819.
Time, 1 April 1969, p. 108.
Sunday Times (London), 1 July 1973, p. 31.
Virginia Quarterly Review, (Summer 1969), p. ci.

D28   "What Is Pornography?" In Perspectives on Pornog-
      raphy. Ed. Douglas A. Hughes. New York: St.
      Martin's, 1970, pp. 4-8.

      Reprint of [G456].

D29   "Words." In Essays by Linguists and Men of Letters
      1858-1964. Vol. 2 of The English Language. Ed.
      Whitney French Bolton and David Crystal. London:
      Cambridge University Press, 1969, pp. 294-304.

      Reprinted from Language Made Plain [D17].

E. WORKS TRANSLATED

E01　CYRANO DE BERGERAC.　By Edmund Rostand.

New York: Knopf, 1971.

Translated from the French and adapted for the modern stage.

Reviews:
　Adams, Phoebe.　Atlantic, January 1972, p. 97.
　Barnes, Clive.　New York Times, 20 September
　　1971, p. 31.
　New York Times Book Review, 26 December 1971,
　　p. 6.

E02　CYRANO DE BERGERAC [Stage production].　By
Edmond Rostand.

Reviews:
　Barnes, Clive.　"Plummer Triumphs in Musical
　　'Cyrano.'"　New York Times 14 May 1973, p. 37.
　"Palace 'Cyrano' Opens March 25."　New York
　　Times, 19 December 1972, p. 56.
　Interview [with Christopher Plummer, who played
　　the lead].　New York Times, 17 May 1973,
　　p. 52.
　Kerr, Walter.　"Cyrano Out of Breath."　New York
　　Times Book Review, 20 May 1973, pp. 1, 35.

E03　THE MAN WHO ROBBED POOR BOXES.　By Jean
Servin.

London: Gollancz, 1965.

Translated from the French Deo Gratias.

44

E04 THE NEW ARISTOCRATS. By Michel de Saint-Pierre.

London: Gollancz, 1962.
Boston: Houghton Mifflin, 1963.

Translated by Anthony and Llewela Burgess from the French Le Nouveaux aristocrates.

E05 OEDIPUS THE KING. By Sophocles.

Minneapolis: University of Minnesota Press, in association with The Guthrie Theater, 1972.

Translated from the Greek and adapted for the modern stage by Anthony Burgess, with comments by Anthony Burgess, Michael Langham, and Stanley Silverman.

Reviews:
 Classical World, 68 (November 1974), p. 211.
 Drama, (Fall 1973), p. 81.

E06 THE OLIVE TREES OF JUSTICE. By Jean Pelegri.

London: Sidgwick and Jackson, 1962.

Translated by Anthony Burgess and Lynn Wilson from the French Le Oliviers de la justice.

F. WORKS EDITED

F01 THE AGE OF THE GRAND TOUR: 1720-1820

London: Elek, 1967.
New York: Crown, 1967.

Edited by Anthony Burgess and Francis Haskell.

Translations:
Mei, Francisco, trans. La Bella Europa [Italian].
    Rome: Editalia, 1970.
Rey, Nicole, Huguette Perrin, and Gloria de
    Cherisey, trans. Le grand siècle du voyage
    [French]. Paris: Michel, 1968.

Reviews:
Canaday, John. "Journey of Diligence." New York
    Times Book Review, 3 December 1967, p. 62.
Ford, B. Burlington Magazine, 110 (August 1968),
    p. 470.
Honour, H. Observer, 8 October 1967, p. 26.
Levey, M. Studio International, 175 (March 1968),
    p. 155.
New Yorker, 9 December 1967, p. 246.
Perreault, John. "More Big 1967 Books." Nation,
    25 December 1967, pp. 696-97.
Rea, Robert. "Travel." Library Journal, 1
    January 1968, p. 77.
Sokolov, R. A. Newsweek, 11 December 1967,
    p. 105.
Time, 15 December 1967, p. 112.
Times Literary Supplement, 8 February 1968,
    p. 135.
Vansittart, Peter. Spectator, 29 December 1967,
    p. 815.
Wall Street Journal, 4 December 1967, p. 20.

F02 THE COACHING DAYS OF ENGLAND: 1750-1850

London: Elek, 1966.
New York: Time-Life, 1966.

Reviews:
Annan, N. New York Review of Books, 18 May
   1967, p. 13.
Hamilton, G. H. Saturday Review, 3 December
   1966, p. 33.
Rea, R. R. Library Journal, 15 February 1967,
   p. 765.
Rosenberg, John D. "Plum Pudding. " Book Week,
   11 December 1966, p. 5.
Showers, Paul. "The Jumble Shelf. " New York
   Times Book Review, 4 December 1966, pp. 38-42.

F03 A JOURNAL OF THE PLAGUE YEAR. By Daniel
Defoe.

Harmondsworth: Penguin, 1966. paper.

Reviews:
Times Literary Supplement, 29 September 1966,
   p. 901.

F04 A SHORTER 'FINNEGANS WAKE. ' By James Joyce.

London: Faber, 1966.
Toronto: Macmillan, 1966.
Seattle: University of Washington Press, 1966.
New York: Viking, 1966. paper.
Toronto: Macmillan, 1968. paper.

Reviews:
Benstock, Bernard. James Joyce Quarterly, 4
   (Winter 1967), pp. 137-39.
Blish, James. Wake Newslitter (Newcastle Univer-
   sity College, N. S. W.), N. S. 3 (August 1966),
   pp. 87-89.
Booklist, 15 April 1967, p. 899.
British Book News, No. 313 (September 1966), p. 716.
Choice, 4 (June 1967), p. 422.
Dublin Magazine, 6 (Spring 1967), p. 94.
Edel, Leon. "A Small Dose of Joyce. " Book

Week, 19 February 1967, pp. 12-13.
Gross, J. Observer, 19 June 1966, p. 26.
Hodgart, Matthew. Guardian, 24 June 1966, p. 11.
————. Manchester Guardian Weekly, 30 June
    1966, p. 11.
Huish, Lois. Library Journal, 1 January 1967,
    p. 134.
Kirkus Service, 1 December 1966, p. 1239.
New York Times Book Review, 1 October 1967,
    p. 38.
Seymour-Smith, Martin. "Burgess's Wake." Spec-
    tator, 24 June 1966, p. 794.
Time, 24 February 1967, p. 92.

G. ARTICLES, ESSAYS, AND REVIEWS

G01   "An Age of Teen." <u>Listener</u>, 16 April 1964, pp. 646-47.

Weekly comments on BBC programs: film study on rootless, alienated young people, for whom compassion is dowsed by the subjects' own whinings and half-baked philosophy that adults had given them nothing to believe in; primitive Brazilians who cling to their suffering God "rather than listen to Communist hucksters who promise an end of hardship"; the eruption of Bald Mountain in Martinique, which killed 40,000 good citizens but "spared a condemned criminal whom man's inhumanity had incarcerated in underground rock. Was that act then good or bad? I feel like sharpening my novelist's pencil about this."

G02   "The Alien Quorn." <u>Listener</u>, 26 March 1964, pp. 530-31.

Weekly comments on BBC programs: the Quorn Society and hunting; the usefulness of an initial teaching alphabet in teaching reading, although such systems lack "genuine linguistic inquiry" and are less logical and economical than the International Phonetic Alphabet; Dr. Alex Comfort's view that "violent art means non-violent living"; potential eavesdropping "far beyond what George Orwell envisaged for twenty years later."

G03   "All About Yves." <u>New York Times Magazine</u>, 11 September 1977, p. 118.

Biographical article on designer Yves St. Laurent.

G04 "Ameringlish Isn't Britglish." New York Times Magazine, 9 September 1973, pp. 86, 88, 93, 95, 100.

Doesn't like and will not adopt hopefully for "one hopes," disinterested to mean "not interested," and split infinitives. "But who am I to proscribe and prescribe? Americans must use language in their own way, and I have no right to appeal to the usages of the mother country." See also the response by Louis Milic [L81].

G05 "Amis and Enemies." Listener, 10 October 1968, p. 475.

Review of I Want It Now, by Kingsley Amis.

G06 "Ana." Guardian, 16 December 1966, p. 7.

Review of Observations, Anecdotes, and Characters of Books and Men, by Joseph Spence, edited by James M. Osborn.

G07 "The Anatomy of Melancholy." Horizon, 12 (Autumn 1970), pp. 48-53.

Describes The Anatomy of Melancholy, by Robert Burton, as the greatest work ever written on melancholy, a never-wearying book from which he is always learning new things.

G08 "Ancient Kickaround (Updated)." Time, 8 July 1974, p. 39.

Comments on the World Cup competition; "football [rugby, soccer, or the American "armored" version] is the only international language, apart from sex."

G09 "Antenatal." Listener, 26 December 1963, pp. 1080-81.

Weekly comments on BBC documentaries: Siberia, a dull country full of dull people who speak interesting, highly agglutinative languages [see G342 for a response to Burgess's comments]; 1963 as a wonderful year for natural disasters; air accidents; a British cathedral to be demolished in order to build a bridge over the river Nile; American decaying executives who must submit to "downward mobility"; a history of Christmas, including a comment on the solecism "ye" for "the" in "Ye Boar's Head."

G10   "Anthony Burgess Meets New York." New York Times Magazine, 29 October 1972, pp. 28, 32, 37-39.

Finds New York, "which is not quite America, simpatico because the place is seething with exiles...." a place where every taste is catered to "appropriate for him because he is not a WASP "but a CASC or Catholic Anglo-Saxon Celt, which makes [him] a kind of Puerto Rican." See also Anne McCormick's response [L77] and Burgess's reply to McCormick [G204].

G11   "Anthony Burgess on Strine." Australian Book Review, 5 (September 1966), pp. 215-16.

Review of The Australian Language, by Sidney Baker.

G12   "The Artist as Martyr." Guardian, 1 September 1967, p. 5.

Review of Flaubert: The Making of the Master, by Enid Starkie.

G13   "The Arts." Listener, 28 May 1964, p. 899.

Review of a performance of La Traviata and the Royal Ballet's Toccata; Paul Tortelier's class on the Elgar cello concerto; a new series, Writer's World, with Dennis Wheatley, L. P. Hartley, Lord David Cecil, Ted Hughes, and Brigid Brophy in the first program; program about Rupert Brooke.

G14   "The Arts." Listener, 23 July 1964, p. 139.

Review of Bartók's Concerto for Orchestra as performed by the Vienna Philharmonic, conducted by
Georg Solti; Benjamin Britten's introduction of his
Cello Symphony to London with Mstislav Rostropovich,
the man he wrote it for: includes a comparison of
changes in musical interpretation with phonemic change
in language; Paul Tortelier playing chamber music at
home with his family; Rachmaninov's Piano Concerto
No. 3 performed by Eugene Moguilevsky, winner of
the Queen Elizabeth piano contest; an interview with
Alfred Hitchcock; a story about a middle-aged Yorkshire factory worker who paints obsessively.

G15   "The Arts." Listener, 20 August 1964, p. 283.

Review of World War I songs and a tribute to Wilfred
Owen; performance of Benjamin Britten's War Requiem;
program of excerpts from Don Giovanni; Larry Adler
playing the harmonica; Brecht on music ("What I don't
like about Brecht is his authoritarianism."); program
on jazz, noting that he once played jazz and pop music
("Jazz is not expressionistic ... it is narcissistic.");
the role of the artist in Siena in the Middle Ages;
Two Old Ladies: Caresse Crosby presiding over a
colony of artists and Mrs. Sterling typing away at her
new book at the age of 96.

G16   "The Arts." Listener, 17 September 1964, p. 441.

Review of Robert Klees's report on the Edinburgh
Festival, with Burgess noting that the most daring
title used in undergraduate theatre was One Hand Clapping from his own novel (1960); performance by Rostropovich of the Schumann Cello Concerto; performance by
Charles Tregor of Mendelssohn Violin Concerto with
the Pittsburgh Symphony Orchestra; performance by
Jacqueline DuPré of Elgar's Cello Concerto; The Yeomen of the Guard, by Gilbert and Sullivan; a program
of Shakespeare discussions; an essay about Edwardian
England, by Carl Brahms; Kitchen Party program, in
which Fanny and Johnnie Cradock served French con-
fection.

G17   "The Arts." Listener, 15 October 1964, p. 603.

Review of a literary documentary on Henrik Ibsen and Emilie Bardach, in which Burgess mentions Finnegans Wake as the great modern prototype for the incest theme; Jocelyn Brooke on the impact of World War II on British writers; production of Iolanthe, by Gilbert and Sullivan; production of The Magic Flute, by Mozart; performance by Yehudi Menuhin of Beethoven concerto, Colin Davis conducting the London Symphony Orchestra; suggests renaming Juke Box Jury the Puke Box Jury.

G18   "The Arts." Listener, 12 November 1964, p. 775.

Review of performance of Mozart's Concerto for Flute, Harp and Orchestra from the Palais Schaezler in Austria; performance by Rostropovich of Bach Suite No. 3; program about Benny Goodman; performance of the Moiseyev Dance Company, about which Burgess notes that "it will take a good deal of psychiatry to locate the trauma which blocks my appreciation of boisterous folksiness"; a note that Burgess appeared on a new panel game about books, entitled, Take It or Leave It.

G19   "The Arts." Listener, 10 December 1964, p. 951.

Review of a program about Winston Churchill, based on his book Painting as a Pastime; Peter Brook interviewed by Jonathan Miller about the production of Marat-Sade; performance of the Bolshoi Opera Company from La Scala, in Milan; Otto Klemperer's interpretation of Beethoven's Choral Symphony; program about Michael Tippett's involvement in the television presentation of his Concerto for Double String Orchestra.

G20   "The Arts." Listener, 7 January 1965, p. 31.

Review of Christmas programs; program with Claude Levi-Strauss on St. Nicholas; program about poet Philip Larkin and New York architect Philip Johnson, who was interviewed by Susan Sontag; the Roayl Ballet's performance of Coppelia described as magnificent; Yehudi Menuhin in teaching sessions and a performance of the Elgar Concerto; a workshop on Shakespeare and music, including a survey of what composers have done with Shakespeare's works.

G21   "The Arts." Listener, 28 January 1965, p. 161.

An obituary for T. S. Eliot, with tributes paid by W. H. Auden, Cleanth Brooks, Michael Tippett, Cyril Connolly, and Henry Moore; a study of Alasdair Gray, an unknown Glasgow poet and painter; a program about Wilfred Josephs, a dentist-composer; Spare the Rod and Spoil the Writer, a program of authors' reminiscences about school, with Burgess's comment that "[I am] exceptional in having learned the important things [to me] out of school. This makes me not quite a British intellectual."

G22   "The Arts." Listener, 18 February 1965, p. 275.

Coverage of Sir Winston Churchill's funeral; performance of the Overture to Die Meistersinger and Brahms Piano Concerto No. 2; a program about Chopin; performance of Beauty and the Beast danced by Doreen Wells and Richard Farley; discusses confusion between spontaneous colloquial speech and "art" speech of drama or oratory in British television.

G23   "The Arts." Listener, 11 March 1965, p. 381.

Discusses how much television critics ought to know about television, concluding that "our concern is with aesthetics, not with technique"; performance of The Firebird by the Royal Ballet; Kenneth MacMillan's Las Hermanas dramatic dance; Verdi's Roman Summer; program about literary exile with Burgess's impression that "one of the inescapable conditions of literary creation is to escape from the mother, no matter how much it hurts"; program on poetry; program concerned with what the artist can learn from science.

G24   "The Arts." Listener, 1 April 1965, p. 499.

Review of a portrait of Sir John Barbirolli; Henry Livings's reasons for writing his plays in Dobcross; Julian Bernart discussing iconic symbols in Africa; the film Time Is, by John Levy; a study of Robert Lowell; an interview with Robert Shaw and David Jones; performance of Prokofiev's Romeo and Juliet, with Yehudi

Menuhin, and Fonteyn and Nureyev dancing the balcony scene.

G25   "The Arts." Listener, 22 April 1965, p. 611.

Review of a talk on Baudelaire by Michael Podro; film about James Joyce (which Burgess narrated and helped produce) reviewed by William Trevor: Silence, Exile and Cunning [G368] is "as close to Joyce and as close to his Dublin as a film of this kind can be"; performance of a youth orchestra; opera singers Evelyn Lear and Thomas Stewart described as "ferociously talented"; a rehearsal program with Paul Tortelier and Denis Matthews working on the last movement of the Beethoven A Major Sonata; Stevie Smith reading poems that "demand to be seen on the page, not heard."

G26   "The Arts." Listener, 13 May 1965, p. 719.

Norman Mailer, Jonathan Miller, and Malcolm Muggeridge in a "three cornered discussion on art and eschatology" that lacked intellectual firmness; discussion between David Daiches and Cleanth Brooks about American and British writers; a program about Dorothy Sayers; end of Shakespeare quatercentenary, with Bosworth Field and repeats of Wars of the Roses and Shakespeare and Music; laudation for Sir Malcom Sargent from Sir Thomas Armstrong, Sir Alan Herbert, and Lord Boothby; performance of Berg's Violin Concerto by Wolfgang Marschner with the BBC symphony.

G27   "The Arts." Listener, 3 June 1965, p. 837.

Review of films about the blues and about Debussy; program about Richard Wagner's Die Götterdämmerung; David Holbrook and an illustrated lecture on the use of poetry.

G28   "At Table." Listener, 7 November 1963, p. 766.

Weekly comments on BBC programs: questions the value of round-table discussions of people answering questions on television, which too often result in a

"choice of two categories only--boors and bores"; criticizes the discussion of Hamlet by actors Peter O'Toole
and Orson Welles; program about the Amazon Indians;
program about pioneer fliers of the 1920s and 1930s,
sacrificial victims and heroes.

G29   "Auden's Minor Birds." Spectator, 11 August 1967,
       pp. 161-62.

       Review of Nineteenth Century Minor Poets, edited by
       W. H. Auden.

G30   "Augustus Carp Addresses a New Generation of Sin-
       ners." Bookseller, 24 September 1966, pp. 1768-
       69.

       An excerpt from his introduction to August Carp, Esq.
       by Himself [D09].

G31   "Authors on Translators." Translation, 2, Nos. 1-2
       (1974), pp. 5-8.

G32   "Away from the Profumeria." Listener, 27 June 1963,
       p. 1086.

       Weekly comments on BBC programs: two programs
       on English politics; a series of four travel programs
       with commentary by Johnny Morris, who "achieves a
       tour de force of dubbing.... The Spanish language is
       turned into comic gibberish; the Spaniards themselves,
       like the Rock apes, can be made to speak Cockney or
       Anglo-Welsh...."; a taut and artistically disciplined
       travel program that depicted "tribal Africa penetrating
       Alexandrian Africa," by Rene Cutworth.

G33   "Bagehot on Books." Spectator, 7 January 1966,
       p. 15.

       Review of The Collected Works of William Bagehot,
       Vols. I and II. Reprinted in Urgent Copy [D27].

G34   "The Battering of Britain." Listener, 6 June 1963,
       pp. 974-75.

       Weekly comments on BBC programs: review of David
       Attenborough's Quest under Capricorn; exposé of colo-
       nialism in Australia; programs dealing with slums and
       substandard housing in England; Allan Taylor's new
       series of lectures.

G35   "Behind the Law." Listener, 27 October 1966, p. 616.

       Review of A Law unto Themselves, by C. Northcote
       Parkinson, archaeologist and historian in Malaya.

G36   "Below the Burma Road." Guardian, 14 April 1967,
       p. 7.

       Review of The Source of the River Kwai, by Pierre
       Boulle, translated by Xan Fielding.

G37   "Beyond the Oxgrove." Spectator, 27 October 1967,
       pp. 493-94.

       Review of A New Canon of English Poetry.

G38   "The Big Daddy of the Beats." Observer Weekend
       Review, 22 May 1966, p. 26.

       Review of Desolation Angels, by Jack Kerouac.

G39   "A Biographer for a Biographer." Guardian, 5 August
       1966, p. 7.

       Review of James Boswell--The Earlier Years, 1740-
       1769, by Frederick A. Pottle; unhesitatingly picks this
       as the book of the year.

G40   "A Bit of a Sissy." Punch, 15 November 1967, p. 757.

       An unfavorable review of The Infirm Glory, Godfrey
       Winn's autobiography, faulting Winn for name-dropping,

poor style, lack of organization, and lack of interest.
See also [G48].

G41   "The Blackness of Whiting. " Spectator, 21 May 1965,
       p. 664.

       Review of three theatrical productions: Saint's Day,
       by Whiting; The Three Sisters, by Chekhov; Mother
       Courage, by Brecht.

G42   "Bless Thee, Bottom...." Times Literary Supplement,
       18 September 1970, pp. 1024-25.

       Discusses the pains and pleasures of translating, a
       legitimate chore for writers who need to earn money.
       Sympathizes with French, German, and Japanese trans-
       lators who have translated his works.   Notes that
       Russians only condemn his works.   See also Michael
       Donley's response [L40].

G43   "Blimey. " New York Times Book Review, 13 August
       1972, pp. 4-5.

       Review of Another Book About London, by Donald God-
       dard.

G44   "Blood in the Matzos. " Spectator, 14 April 1967,
       p. 424.

       Review of The Fixer, The Assistant, and A New Life,
       by Bernard Malamud. Reprinted in Urgent Copy
       [D27].

G45   "Blues for Mr. Baldwin. " Spectator, 14 May 1965,
       pp. 632-33.

       Review of three theatrical productions: Blues for Mr.
       Charlie, The Solid Gold Cadillac, and Portrait of a
       Queen.

G46   "Boo. " New York Times Book Review, Part II, 11
       February 1973, pp. 2, 24-26.

See response from J. Cleworth [L28].

G47   "The Book Is Not for Reading." New York Times
       Book Review, 4 December 1966, pp. 1, 74.

       About books he should have read as a youth, books by
       Jane Austen, Sir Walter Scott, H. G. Wells; enjoys
       reading that is strongly male-oriented; concludes that
       the adult absorbs what is read, but the youth is ab-
       sorbed by it.

G48   "Books They Liked Best and Books They Liked Least."
       Book World, 3 December 1967, pp. 16-17.

       Burgess's choices for 1967: Books he liked best--
       Poems of Gerard Manley Hopkins; The Ambidextrous
       Universe, by Martin Gardner; and The Scope of An-
       thropology, by Claude Levi-Strauss [G166]; book he
       liked least--The Infirm Glory, by Godfrey Winn [G40].
       The choices of Herman Kahn [L66] included Burgess's
       A Clockwork Orange and The Wanting Seed in the
       books-liked-best category.

G49   "Books Wanted in 1967: A Dream of Publishing."
       Times (London), 2 February 1967, p. 16.

       First in a series of articles in which writers discuss
       books they would like to see published--or republished:
       (1) an Augustan satire in impeccable heroic couplets;
       (2) a novel written entirely in carefully disguised Pe-
       trarchan sonnets; (3) The Sexual Cycle of Human War-
       fare, by Norman Walters; (4) Fowler's End, by Ger-
       ald Kersh; (5) There's a Porpoise Close Behind Us,
       by Noel Langley.

G50   "The Brotherhood." Spectator, 27 January 1967,
       pp. 106-07.

       Review of Rossetti and the Pre-Raphaelite Brotherhood,
       by G. H. Fleming; Millais and the Ruskins, by Mary
       Lutyens; The Professor (Arthur Severns's Memoir of
       John Ruskin), edited by James S. Dearden. Reprinted
       in Urgent Copy [D27].

G51   "Burgess on Kubrick on 'Clockwork. '" Library Journal,
        1 May 1973, p. 1506.

        Review of Stanley Kubrick's A Clockwork Orange:
        Based on the Novel by Anthony Burgess [A05]. A
        review in the dialect Nadsat signed by "Alex" (a
        character from the novel).

G52   "Burgess, Originator of 'Clockwork, ' Says 'Let Kubrick
        Defend Film. '" Variety, 22 August 1973, pp. 2,
        40.

        Thinks the film "is a truly remarkable work, and is
        as truthful an interpretation of my own book as I could
        ever hope to find" but is exasperated by people who
        expect him to defend the film. Same as review [A05].

G53   "Camus at His Exercises." Guardian, 18 February
        1966, p. 7.

        Review of Carnets 1942-1951, by Albert Camus, trans-
        lated and annotated by Philip Thody.

G54   "Candid Camera." Spectator, 18 February 1966,
        p. 201.

        Review of Exhumantions, by Christopher Isherwood.

G55   "Caprine Messiah." Spectator, 31 March 1967, p. 369.

        Review of Giles Goat-Boy, by John Barth. Reprinted
        in Urgent Copy [D27].

G56   "Carry On Jack." Observer Weekend Review, 18
        September 1966, p. 26.

        Review of The Moment and Other Pieces, by J. B.
        Priestley.

G57   "Cast a Cold Eye." Spectator, 15 January 1975,
        p. 73.

Article on W. B. Yeats and reviews of The Vast Design: Patterns in W. B. Yeats' Aesthetic, by Edward Engeberg; W. B. Yeats: Selected Criticism, edited by A. Norman Jeffares; and Yeats, by Peter Ure. Reprinted in Urgent Copy [D27].

G58   "A Chekhov for Ireland?" Spectator, 18 December 1964, p. 848.

Review of Collection Two, by Frank O'Connor.

G59   "Choosing to Die." Times Literary Supplement, 14 January 1977, p. 33.

Review of Black Sun, by Geoffrey Wolff.

G60   "Clockwork Marmalade." Listener, 17 February 1972, pp. 197-99.

Compliments Stanley Kubrick's A Clockwork Orange [A05]. Explains that the phrase "clockwork orange" first came to his attention in the speech of an elderly Cockney man, that his novel, on which Kubrick's film is based, was intended to be a tract on "the importance of the power of choice" and "a brainwashing primer," that the invented dialect Nadsat of the novel and the movie is an important aspect of the brainwashing, and that he does not like this novel as much as others he has written.

G61   "Cloud-Cuckoo-Land." Spectator, 23 April 1965, p. 563.

Review of the theatrical production of The Birds, by Vassilis Rota, produced and directed by Karolos Koun. Based on Aristophanes' Ornithes.

G62   "Cobblers." Spectator, 19 March 1965, p. 364.

Review of two theatrical productions, Hobson's Choice and Happy End.

G63   "A Colonial Christmas." Punch, 4 December 1968,
       pp. 801-02.

       Describes a wacky Christmas day in Malaya, including
       visits by such guests as a black magician and a prosti-
       tute and a dousing in an ocean abounding with croco-
       diles.

G64   "Coming Soon: Hilton-upon-Stratford." New York
       Times, 11 March 1971, p. 43.

G65   "Coming to the Crunch." Guardian, 4 November 1966,
       p. 6.

       Review of Nature and Human Nature, by Alex Comfort.
       A survey of the human situation and how it came about.

G66   "Commercials." Listener, 2 November 1967, pp. 583-
       84.

       Discusses the success and the effect of commercials,
       citing Marshall McLuhan, in relation to The Prisoner,
       a new program that absorbed commercial techniques
       into entertainment. Review of a television production
       of Aldous Huxley's After Many a Summer, adapted by
       Rex Tucker; A Black Candle for Mr. Gogarty; and
       Man Alive: No Fixed Abode.

G67   "Concerning Amation." Guardian, 10 July 1964, p. 7.

       Review of Erotic Poetry, edited by William Cole, with
       a foreword by Stephen Spender, and A Literary Guide
       to Seduction, edited by Robert Meister, with an intro-
       duction by Leslie A. Fiedler.

G68   "The Corruption of the Exotic." Listener, 26 Septem-
       ber 1963, pp. 465-67.

       Began writing his novels in response to exotic Malaya,
       a land with strange and glamorous subject matter.
       Claims that the aesthetic impulse should provide the
       inspiration for a writer rather than strange and exotic

subject matter. Discusses D. H. Lawrence's Kangaroo and The Plumed Serpent as exotic novels. Claims that novelists today have the areas of language and myth available, noting that William Golding's The Inheritors uses language to suggest "a world before language existed," but that Golding's Lord of the Flies and Iris Murdoch's A Severed Head allow content or myth to become more important than the novelist's technique.

G69 "Coves and Morts." Guardian, 19 March 1965, p. 11.

G70 Cream and Offal." Spectator, 13 November 1964, p. 643.

Review of a rather unconnected batch of books: Girls in Their Married Bliss, by Edna O'Brien; Better Dead than Red, by Stanley Reynolds; One Man, One Matchet, by T. M. Aluko; The Cool Meridian, by Sarah Kilpatrick; and The Main Experiment, by Christopher Hodder Williams.

G71 "Crisis in Gibraltar." Spectator, 23 April 1965, p. 528.

An argument presented to the British people for the retention of Gibraltar as a British colony: the Gibraltarians themselves prefer British influence; they fear Franco's Spain.

G72 "Culture as a Hot Meal." Spectator, 11 July 1970, pp. 13-14.

Review of The Raw and the Cooked, by Claude Levi-Strauss, translated by John Weightman and Doreen Weightman.

G73 "Curry and Claret." Listener, 8 September 1966, p. 360.

Burgess defends Britain's colonizing of Singapore in reviewing two historical source books: An Anecdotal

64 / Anthony Burgess: A Bibliography

History of Old Times in Singapore, by Charles Burton
Buckley, and Our Tropical Possessions in Malayan
India, by John Cameron.

G74   "Cyrano de Bergerac: Part of a Draft Translation."
       Malahat Review, No. 17 (January 1971), pp. 81-89.

G75   "Daltonian Prejudice." Guardian, 16 November 1966,
       p. 20.

       Explains the problem of being color blind from his own
       color-blind perspective. Criticizes the use of color
       symbolism for categorization and the State's sponsoring
       a reading method based on color recognition.

G76   "Damned Dot...." Guardian, 21 December 1966,
       p. 12.

       A defense of the British money system, including crit-
       icism of the totalitarian decimal money system.

G77   "Dare to Be a Catman." Spectator, 15 March 1968,
       pp. 330-31.

       Review of A Dictionary of Cat Lovers, by Christobel
       Lady Abercomways, with biographical references to
       his own cat and Malaya.

G78   "Dark Disease as a European Tradition." Common-
       weal, 13 May 1966, pp. 231-32.

       A brief and favorable review of Incubus (Male Oscuro),
       by Giuseppe Berto, with a longer discussion of the
       novel as distinctly European rather than American and
       some of the differences between contemporary Italian
       and American literature. Reprinted in Urgent Copy
       [D27].

G79   "Dear Mr. Shame's Voice." Spectator, 27 November
       1964, pp. 731-32.

Review of Joyce's "Portrait": Criticisms and Critiques, edited by Thomas Connolly; A New Approach to Joyce, by Robert S. Ryf; The Art of James Joyce, by A. Walton Litz; and Joyce's Benefictions, by Helmut Bonheim.

Reprinted as "Joyce Industry in the U. S. " [G188]. Also reprinted in Urgent Copy [D27].

G80   "Déjà Vu. " Listener, 7 September 1967, pp. 315-16.

Weekly comments on BBC programs: The Big M, by Lester Powell; Michael Ayston's talk about Degas' The Laundresses; a program about conflict between traditional and "with it" morality; a program about the Concorde; Morley Safer on the brainwashing of Chinese children against the West; a program of rock and roll music that horrifies Burgess; an intellectual game show.

G81   "The Democracy of Prejudice. " Encounter, 29 (August 1967), pp. 71-75.

Review of Fifty Works of English Literature We Could Do Without, by Brigid Brophy, Michael Levey, and Charles Osborne. Reprinted in Urgent Copy [D27].

G82   "Depraved Humanity. " Guardian, 31 March 1966, pp. 5-6.

Review of Rogue's Progress: An Autobiography of "Lord Chief Daron" Nicholson, edited by John L. Bradley.

G83   "Dickens Loud and Clear. " Spectator, 23 December 1966, p. 817.

Review of Oliver Twist, edited by Kathleen Tillotson. The Clarendon Dickens. General editors John Butt and Kathleen Tillotson. Reprinted in Urgent Copy [D27].

G84   "Did Shakespeare Mean That, Or Is It a Printer's

Error?" Chicago Tribune Book World, 12 January 1969, p. 5.

Review of The First Folio of Shakespeare, prepared by Charlton Hinman.

G85   "Dirty Words." New York Times Magazine, 8 August 1976, p. 6.

Claims that it is useless, and worse, harmful to try to purge taboo and obscene words and epithets from the English language. See responses by Helene Hanff [L57], Nancy Swann [L113], and Sheila Taub [L115].

G86   "Discussing 'Coronation Street.'" Listener, 10 August 1967, pp. 186-87.

Weekly comments on BBC programs: programs about an air crash in Tokyo Bay; a young woman in a geriatric hospital because of the National Health Service; an examination of social instincts; avante garde films; and Dennis Potter's play, Where the Buffalo Roams.

G87   "Dr. Rowse Meets Dr. Faustus." Nation, 1 February 1965, pp. 115, 117-18.

Review of Christopher Marlowe: His Life and Work, by A. L. Rowse. Mentions that he (Burgess) wrote a graduation thesis about Marlowe in Manchester, England. Same as "Dr. Rowstus," in Urgent Copy [D27].

G88   "Don't Cook Mother Goose." New York Times Book Review, 5 November 1967, Part 2 (Children's Books), pp. 1, 48, 50.

Defends Mother Goose nursery rhymes as more literary and more appropriate for children than their modern competition, the commercial television ad.

G89   "Durrell and the Homunculi." Saturday Review, 21 March 1970, pp. 29-31.

Review of Numquam, by Lawrence Durrell.

G90   "Easter 1964." Listener, 2 April 1964, pp. 566-67.

Weekly comments on BBC programs: a documentary
about air pilots; an appraisal of Becket's personality
in fiction (T. S. Eliot and Jean Anouilh) and in history
(Professor Galbraith); a program about Jane Goodall's
study of primates; Patrick O'Donovan's look at Ireland
with reference to W. B. Yeats; Michael Flanders and
Donald Swann reading from the New English Bible and
singing Sydney Carter's carols.

G91   "Easy Money: Brought with the Wind." Punch, 25
        September 1968, pp. 428-30.

A ten-shilling note found in the street increases through
gambling luck to 40,000 pounds, which was invested in a
publishing firm but blown away on a libel suit contest-
ing some unimportant segment in the life story of a
rock star.   Discovers that the ten-shilling note was
hiw own, dropped from his pocket.   Ends with a plea
for ten-shilling notes so that he can continue his study
of luck.

G92   "An Electric Grape." American Scholar, 35 (Autumn
        1966), pp. 719-20.

An invited response to the Spring 1966 issue of American Scholar: A positive reaction particularly to the
articles by Roger Wescott about contemporary linguistics, Joseph Krutch about cybernetics, and Marshall
McLuhan about popular culture.   Concludes that he is
wary of a scientific era that threatens his culture and
his independence: "Professor McLuhan's electric
grapes can so far only impart some very sour shocks;
I await the treading and the vintage."

G93   "The Emigrants." Punch, 12 June 1968, pp. 852-54.

G94   "Enduring Saturday." Spectator, 29 April 1966,
        pp. 532-33.

Review of The Testament of Samuel Beckett, by Josephine Jacobsen and William R. Mueller. Reprinted in Urgent Copy [D27].

G95   "Enemy of Twilight." Spectator, 22 July 1966, p. 124.

Review of Collected Works, by J. M. Synge, Vol. II: Prose, edited by Alan Price. Reprinted in Urgent Copy [D27].

G96   "English as an America." Encounter, 278 (February 1967), pp. 67-71.

Review of Modern American Usage, by Wilson Follet, edited and completed by Jacques Barzun and others, and The Random House Dictionary of the English Language. Criticizes Follet's purgative approach to typical Americanisms and the dictionary's continuing the use of old-fashioned diacritical marks in the pronunciation guide instead of the more accurate and useful International Phonetic Alphabet. "These people have no more authority to legislate for usage than you or I or anyone.... If we go to Fowler or Follet for guidance, it should be in the narrow zone of linguistic etiquette on which--in our superstitious way--we are always reaoy to be instructed, as in movements of a religious ritual." Reprinted in Urgent Copy [D27].

G97   "Enjoying Walton." Listener, 6 June 1968, pp. 750-51.

Review of programs about the British composer Walton; California nuns shedding their habits for civilian clothes; American politics; and the opera star Geraint Evans.

G98   "Entente Concordiale." Listener, 9 April 1964, pp. 602-03.

Weekly comments on BBC programs: the intrinsic and extrinsic problems of building the Concorde; The Face of Christ program, by Reverend Anthony Bridges, who is also a painter; the Oxford Revue about capital punishment; a study of Tennyson; a program about the distinction between Mods and Rockers.

G99   "Et Ego in Arcadia. " Spectator, 4 August 1967, pp. 133-34.

Review of O Canada: An American's Notes on Canadian Culture, by Edmund Wilson.

G100 "Europe's Day of the Dead. " Spectator, 20 January 1967, p. 74.

Review of Under the Volcano, by Malcolm Lowry, and The Letters of Malcolm Lowry, edited by Harvey Breit and Margerie Bonner Lowry.

G101 "Evelyn Waugh, 1903-1966: The Comedy of Ultimate Truths. " Spectator, 15 April 1966, p. 462.

Eulogy for Evelyn Waugh. Reprinted as "The Comedy of Ultimate Truths" in Urgent Copy [D27].

G102 "Exhausted Wells. " Spectator, 28 January 1966, p. 111.

Review of H. G. Wells--Journalism and Prophecy, 1893-1946, edited by W. Warren Wagar.

G103 "A Fable for Social Scientists. " Horizon, 15 (Winter 1973), pp. 12-15.

B. F. Skinner, behavioral conditioning, and free will. See also W. Karp's "The Clockwork Society" [L67].

G104 "Fed Up to Here. " Letter. New York Times Book Review, 20 October 1966, pp. 66-67.

See also responses by B. H. Fussell [L50] and D. E. Waldo [L121].

G105 "The First J. J." Spectator, 18 March 1966, p. 332.

Review of Twelve and a Tilly (essays on the occasion of the 25th anniversary of Finnegans Wake), edited by Jack B. Dalton and Clive Hart; A Question of Modernity (essays on writing with special reference to Joyce and Beckett), by Anthony Cronin; and James Joyce in Paris: His Final Years, by Gisele Freund and V. B. Carleton.

G106 "The First Madame Bovary." Spectator, 30 September 1966, p. 414.

Review of November, by Gustave Flaubert. Reprinted in Urgent Copy [D27].

G107 "Fleurs du Mal." Spectator, 9 September 1966, p. 326.

Review of The Reactionaries, by John Harrison. Reprinted in Urgent Copy [D27].

G108 "Flimsy Pretexts." Listener, 23 January 1964, pp. 166-67.

Weekly comments on BBC programs: report on West German/British studies of the correlation of smoking and lung cancer; a survey of automation and an era of more pay and greater leisure; a program about the problems of communication in three London schools in which there are children from fourteen different races; Balloon Over the Alps--a play about the automated future; the problems of dispersing troops to the trouble spots in the Commonwealth.

G109 "Focus on Theatre." Harper's Bazaar, April 1973, pp. 98, 128.

G110 "For Love or Money." Newsweek, 4 June 1973, p. 62.

G111   "For Permissiveness, with Misgivings." New York
        Times Magazine, 1 July 1973, pp. 19-20.

        Comments on the Supreme Court ruling on obscenity.
        Argues that writers and filmmakers must be free to
        write and produce their works without restrictions.
        Agrees with the view of "total permissiveness," but
        raises the question of who will do the permitting. See
        response from W. Gleneak [L53].

G112   "Formidable Navigators." Listener, 15 August 1963,
        p. 250.

        Comments on BBC documentaries: a manufacturing
        executive; airport and bridge construction workers;
        state encouragement of sport.

G113   "Fraynetic." Guardian, 22 January 1965, p. 7.

        Review of The Tin Men, by Michael Frayn.

G114   "The Freedom We Have Lost." Time, 8 May 1978,
        pp. 44, 49.

        Discusses today's terrorism and democracy, with
        comments on the recent increase in violence and ag-
        gression.

G115   "Frenglish." Encounter, 30 (June 1968), pp. 75-77.

        Review of Mots d'Heures, by Luis Dantin van Rooten.
        A book for those who love macaronics and the mystery
        of words.

G116   "From A to ZZZ." New York Times Book Review,
        21 September 1969, pp. 2, 51.

G117   "From the Inside." Guardian, 29 January 1965, p. 10.

        Review of The Working Novelist, by V. S. Pritchett.

G118 "Funferall." Guardian, 15 July 1966, p. 8.

Review of Joyce-Again's Wake, by Bernard Benstock, and The Joyce Paradox, by Arnold Goldman.

G119 "The Future of Anglo-American." Harper's, February 1968, pp. 53-56.

Notes that technological trends in society and increasing abstraction in language often result in "gobbledygook," which is a way of disguising lies. Deplores vagueness in language but is not conservative toward change in English. Believes that American English rather than British English is providing a speech norm for both the present and the future. Endorses the concept of a common form of the language, or a unified English--Anglo-American.

G120 "Gash-Gold/Vermillion." Spectator, 22 September 1967, pp. 326-27. Reprinted in Urgent Copy [D27].

Review of Complete Poems, by Gerard Manley Hopkins. 4th ed. Reprinted in Urgent Copy [D27].

G121 "Germans and Other Absurdities." Saturday Review, 22 July 1978, p. 58.

G122 "Gerontion." Listener, 14 November 1963, pp. 804-05.

Weekly comments on BBC documentaries: programs about the aged and about Sicily; a program about the rescue of eleven trapped miners contrasted with a rehearsal for "Miss World 1963"; and a summer program, The Buskers of Marrakesh, which had influenced Burgess to see the Djemas el Fna on his vacation.

G123 "Ghost at the Wedding." Spectator, 7 May 1965, pp. 599-602.

Theatrical review of The Dybbuk, directed by Zui Friedland.

G124 "Gibraltar." Holiday, February 1967, pp. 70-71, 86-
87, 92-93, 126-27, 129.

Writes about Spain's desire to annex Gibraltar and the
Gibraltarians' desire to remain a British colony. Includes autobiographical reference to his first experiences
there as a non-commissioned officer during World War
II. Also includes anecdotes about the apes of Gibraltar.

G125 "Gladly My (Maltese George) Cross I'd Bear." Punch,
10 June 1970, pp. 860-61.

Describes Malta as a tax haven and a culture vacuum.
Comments on Maltese attitudes toward settlers, religion,
birds, food, the big city, and censorship. Relates that
a French translation of one of his books, Tremor of
Intent [A28], with the title, Un Agent qui vous vent du
bien, was confiscated by Maltese authorities, while a
Danish translation entitled Martyrernes Blod was
speedily forwarded to him.

G126 "Glamour Under the Elms." Travel and Leisure
(October-November 1971), pp. 6, 10.

Discusses his experiences as and his views of a visiting professor of creative writing.

G127 "God in the Gaps." Listener, 28 October 1963,
pp. 668-69.

Weekly comments on BBC documentaries: a biographical program about Alec Home, narrated by Robin Day
and Robert Mackenzie; a program about Lord Boothby's life; a program about Reuben Green, an eighty-
six-year-old charmer and bus conductor; and a program about the rare snowy owls and musk-oxen.

G128 "The God of the Beatles." Listener, 9 October 1967,
pp. 447-48.

Weekly comments on BBC documentaries: David Frost
talk with Beatles George Harrison and John Lennon

about the Maharishi Silent Song; Lady Windemere's Fan; the story of Queen Mary; a program about the blind; and a National Youth Theatre Production.

G129   "Golding Unbuttoned." Listener, 4 November 1965, pp. 717-18.

Review of The Hot Gales, by William Golding.

G130   "The Good Companion." Spectator, 17 November 1967, pp. 609-10.

Review of The Oxford Companion to English Literature, by Sir Paul Harvey. Reprinted in Urgent Copy [D27].

G131   "A Good Man Destroyed--Hilariously." Life, 15 March 1968, p. 8.

Review of Cocksure, by Mordecai Richler. A very funny book that Burgess wishes he had written himself.

G132   "A Good Read." New York Times Book Review, 15 June 1969, pp. 2, 42-43.

G133   "The Gospel According to Anthony Burgess." New York Times, 3 April 1977, Arts Section, pp. 1, 36.

Burgess on his screenplay for Jesus of Nazareth, a six-hour film for television directed by Franco Zeffirelli. See also "Zeffirelli to Direct a TV Life of Christ" [L126] and his article in Our Sunday Visitor [G305].

G134   "Graham Greene." Encyclopaedia Brittanica, Vol. 10, 1969, pp. 892-93.

G135   "Graham Greene as Monsieur Vert." Tablet, 15 March 1975, pp. 259-60.

G136 "A Grave Matter." Listener, 13 June 1963, p. 1012.

Weekly comments on BBC programs: includes comments on a film biography of Pope John; a history of the Profumo affair; a documentary (The Proud African) by Patrick O'Donovan, who combines a fine script with brilliant patchwork of film techniques to provide a profile of Kwame Nkrumah; a study of science fiction films; and a revivalist religious group.

G137 "Graves and Omar." Encounter, 30 (January 1968), pp. 77-80.

Review of The Rubaiyat of Omar Khayyam, translated by Robert Graves and Omar Ali-Shah. Compares Fitzgerald's translation with this new translation, concluding that Graves's effort is closer in meaning to the Persian poem, but it is poetically pedestrian. Reprinted in Urgent Copy [D27].

G138 "The Great American Visionary." Spectator, 25 March 1966, p. 365.

Review of Leaves of Grass, by Walt Whitman, edited by Harold W. Blodgett and Sculley Bradley.

G139 "The Great Gangster." Listener, 17 March 1966, p. 401.

Review of The Anti-Death League, by Kingsley Amis.

G140 "Great Mogul Beethoven--Genius Got in the Way." Vogue, 15 March 1970, pp. 132-33.

Compares the artist Beethoven with Samuel Johnson, applauds his unorthodoxy in his art and toward his audience, and equates the Beethovenian with the Napoleonic spirit. Beethoven saved from being a minor musician by his genius in these areas.

G141 "The Great Vowel Shift and All That." Encounter, 26 (May 1966), pp. 70-73.

Review of The Story of Language, 2nd edition, by
Mario Pei. Discusses philology, semantic change, and
phonological change in the context of the review. Explains the different views of the student of literature
and the philologist toward language.

G142 "The Grimm Brothers." Horizon, 10 (Winter 1968),
pp. 66-72.

A capsule biography of Jacob and Wilhelm Grimm in
relation to their collection of German folk tales. Explains philological analysis for the general reader and
Jacob Grimm's law of sound change in the Germanic
languages. Reprinted as "Snow White and Rose Red"
in Urgent Copy [D27].

G143 "Growing Up an Only Child." New York Times, 15
June 1977, Sect. C, pp. 1, 11.

See also F. St. Sauveur's response [L103].

G144 "Guide to G. B. S." Observer Weekend Review, 30
January 1966, p. 27.

Review of Shaw in His Time, by Ivor Brown.

G145 "Guilt." Listener, 29 August 1963, pp. 322-23.

Weekly comments on BBC documentaries: a week of
guilt and shame: querulous German attitude about the
poor image the press projects of them; the Negro
march on Washington, with fierce speeches by Malcolm
X and James Baldwin; story about breeding pheasants
to be shot by rich men in West India; an obituary on
Lord Nuffield; a program about Yehudi Menuhin and
Shri Iyengar.

G146 "Gun and Pen." Spectator, 7 July 1967, pp. 15-16.

Review of Blasting and Bombadiering, by Wyndham
Lewis.

G147   "He Wrote Good." Spectator, 8 July 1966, p. 47.

Review of Papa Hemingway, by A. E. Hotchner. Reprinted in Urgent Copy [D27].

G148   "Here Parla Man Marcommunish." Spectator, 25
November 1966, pp. 674-75.

Discusses the linguistic process of language mixing,
e. g. , Franglais and the exporting of English words.
Speculates on the linguistic effects of Britain's joining
the Common Market.

G149   "Here's to Me and My Generation--Mr. Burgess Makes
a Christmas Toast. " New York Times Magazine,
24 December 1972, pp. 4-5, 17.

G150   "H. G. Wells: Seeing the Shape of Things to Come. "
New York Times Book Review, 3 August 1969,
pp. 1, 18.

Review of His Turbulent Life and Times, by Lovat
Dickson.

G151   "Hic et Ubique. " Listener, 23 April 1964, pp. 694-95.

Weekly comments on BBC programs: Khrushchev at
seventy, the exporting of weapons, Les Halles in
Paris, discussion of Camus' Caligula.

G152   "Hindu Crush. " Spectator, 16 June 1967, p. 714.

Review of A Meeting by the River, by Christopher
Isherwood.

G153   "His Ain Folk. " Spectator, 11 November 1966,
p. 621.

Review of The Company I've Kept: Essays in Autobiography, by Hugh MacDiarmid.

G154 "Homage to Barcelona." New York Times Magazine,
4 December 1977, pp. 44-45.

Provides a verbal tour of this cultural and linguistic
maverick, the "Paris of the Mediterranean"; observes
that literature needs to return to unofficial language
and dialects, in which writers can escape the abstrac-
tions of official language.

G155 "Home Thoughts." Listener, 27 February 1964,
pp. 368-69.

Weekly comments on BBC programs: Evelyn Waugh
interviewed by Elizabeth Jane Howard; celebration of
quatercentenaries of Galileo and Michelangelo; a program about India's population problem contrasted with
a program about the problem of infertility; an interview with four mathematicians; and a local cultural
feast in Belfast.

G156 "Homo Aquaticus." Listener, 25 July 1963, p. 142.

Weekly comments on BBC programs: Jacques Cousteau
and hydrospheres, with a personal note by Burgess
that his own fear of water made his viewing the program a painful experience; a student at the Royal Acad-
emy School of Art; Siamese dancing; horses; and a
program about the flittermouse narrated by Wilfred
Hyde White and Robert Morley.

G157 "Homo Sibilans." Times Literary Supplement, 21
January 1977, p. 65.

G158 "Honoring a Prophet in His Own Country." Triquar-
terly, 19 (Fall 1970), pp. 60-62.

Burgess's contribution to an issue dedicated to Edward
Dahlberg, in which he searches for the clue to Dahlberg's lack of popularity in America in his analysis
of Dahlberg's work.

G159 "How I Wrote My Third Symphony." New York Times,

28 December 1975, Arts and Leisure Section, pp. 1, 17.

G160   "How Often Is Diurnal?" Listener, 12 March 1964, p. 444.

Weekly comments on BBC programs: a European journal with a report on Gaston Defferre, an account of Europe's cultural influence on America, and a study of displaced persons in Germany; a program about a Brittania crash at Innsbruck, the future of the Greek monarchy, and Chou En-lai in Pakistan; Ada Reeve (facing her ninetieth birthday and working on a new film), a lion tamer, and the Chinese tops of the pops ("I Love Chairman Mao," "Our Communal Dining-Hall," and "Our Bumper Harvest"); Alan Whicker in Trinidad.

G161   "How Well Have They Worn? Ulysses." Times (London), 17 March 1966, p. 15.

Review of Ulysses, by James Joyce. Describes the book as almost the last of the great serialized novels, a book that reflects the glory of family relationships reflected in the stability of larger communities, and Joyce's reveling in a special and appropriate literary technique--conducting a ritual rather than telling a story. Reprinted as "Ulysses: How Well Has It Worn?" in Urgent Copy [D27].

G162   "The Human Russians." Listener, 28 December 1961, pp. 1107-08.

Expected to find in Leningrad a Russian "steel-and-stone image of the Orwellian future," but instead found the Russians to be humanly inefficient--lying, serving dinner hours late, suffering from depression and drunkenness. Observes that the efficiency that produces sputniks is "a thin cream floated to the top ... far away from the homely smell of blocked up drains and borshch." Same as [G163].

G163   "Human Russians." Science Digest, May 1962, pp. 33-37.

Reprint of "The Human Russians, " [G162].

G164   "Humor and the Real. " Guardian, 30 November 1966,
        p. 16.

Criticizes the ignorance and inverted snobbery often
implicit in light entertainment, its "lowbrow fallacies"
being the "basis of much bad comedy. " Uses My Fair
Lady, as a musical adaptation of George Bernard
Shaw's Pygmalion, as an example.

G165   "Idiophone Book. " Times Literary Supplement, 11
        February 1965, p. 112. [unsigned]

G166   "If Oedipus Had Read His Levi-Strauss. " Book World,
        26 November 1967, p. 6.

Review of The Scope of Anthropology, by Claude Levi-
Strauss. Compares an Algonquin and Iroquois Indian
myth recounted in the book to the Oedipus myth and
links the puzzle-solving aspect of the myth to the
sexual taboo on incest. An important background
reading for Burgess's novel MF [A21]. Reprinted in
Urgent Copy [D27].

G167   "In Defense of William Burroughs. " Letter. Times
        Literary Supplement, 2 January 1964, p. 10.

See also letters by Nicholas Bentley [L14], David
Damant [L35], Wilson Harris [L58], and Wilson Plant
[L93].

G168   "In Search of Shakespeare the Man. " Listener, 23
        April 1964, pp. 670-71.

Contrasts his vision of Shakespeare's love life with
John Manningham's anecdote describing Shakespeare as
a witty lecher. Observes that Shakespeare was per-
sonally shy of involvement with the world, sought a
purgation of fleshly attachments in his plays, and
wrote his plays to make money rather than to leave
timeless plays for posterity. See also Nothing Like
the Sun [A24] and Shakespeare [D26]. Reprinted in
Urgent Copy [D27].

G169 "In the Other England, the Land of Cotton, Nobody Says 'Baaaaath.'" New York Times, 28 January 1973, Resort and Travel Section, p. 1.

An article about the life and dialect of Lancashire. See also the letters by L. Rebanks [L98], S. L. Johnson [L64], Mrs. R. N. Manning [L79], N. Halebsky [L54], and Otto Janssen [L63]. See also Burgess's response, "Pubbing and Dubbing in the Baaaaalmy 'Other England'" [G337].

G170 "In the Year of Jubilee." Times Literary Supplement, 11 February 1977, p. 147.

Review of Majesty, by Robert Lacey. See response from Zacharias Thundy [L116].

G171 "Information About Augustus Carp, Esq." Times Literary Supplement, 15 July 1965, p. 602.

A request for information about this book and its author. See also [D09].

G172 "Inspired Mismanagement." Listener, 30 January 1964, pp. 208-09.

G173 "Inting." Saturday Review, August 1978, p. 62.

G174 "Involvement: Writers Reply." London Magazine, August 1968, p. 9.

G175 "Iridectomy." Guardian, 11 September 1964, p. 10.

Review of The Italian Girl, by Iris Murdoch.

G176 "The Irish in Me." Guardian, 7 December 1966, p. 16.

G177 "Irritation." Listener, 26 September 1963, pp. 482-83.

G178 "Is America Falling Apart?" New York Times Magazine, 7 November 1971, pp. 99-104.

Same as [D15].

G179 "Is Italy a Burnt-Out Case?" Saturday Review, 24 June 1978, p. 46.

G180 "Is Shakespeare Relevant?" New York Times, 11 December 1970, p. 47.

G181 "Italus the Swabian." Guardian, 13 May 1966, p. 8.

Review of Italo Svevo: The Man and the Writer, by P. N. Furbank.

G182 "Japanese Pillow Pattern." Spectator, 22 December 1967, pp. 782-83.

Review of The Pillow Book of Sei Shonagun, translated and edited by Ivan Morris.

G183 "The Jew as American." Spectator, 17 October 1966, pp. 455-56.

A review essay about Dangling Man, The Victim, The Adventures of Augie March, Henderson the Rain King, Seize the Day, and Herzog, by Saul Bellow; the Jew achieving self-realization in America; and Bellow's language as the contribution of the cultivated American Jew. Reprinted in Urgent Copy [D27].

G184 "John Bull's Other Language." Punch, 6 January 1971, pp. 18-19.

Concerned with the difficulty of the literary life in Ireland, where telling stories instead of writing them is a great temptation. Comments on the Irish provincialism and the lack of appreciation for Irish writers.

G185   "Johnson (?) on Johnson." Horizon, 10 (Summer
            1968), pp. 60-64.

        A Burgessian addition to Samuel Johnson's Lives of the
        Poets.

G186   "Joyce Can't Really Be Imitated. ..." Books and
            Bookmen, 15, No. 10 (July 1970), pp. 8-9.

        Discusses James Joyce, Gerard Manley Hopkins, and
        Rudyard Kipling in terms of their use of language.
        Notes that Joyce cannot be imitated because to do so
        is to imitate the content of his work. Compares the
        musical scale to the vowel system of language. Claims
        that using plain language violates the genius of language.

G187   "Joyce Cary's Heroic Journey Up." Life, 25 October
            1968, p. 15.

        Review of Joyce Cary, by Malcolm Forster; describes
        it as a sound but pedestrian book.

G188   "The Joyce Industry in the United States." Atlas, 10
            (July-August 1965), pp. 51-53.

        Reprint of "Dear Mr. Shame's Voice" [G79].

G189   "Jubilate." Listener, 5 March 1964, pp. 406-07.

        Weekly comments on BBC programs: a program about
        viruses by Dr. Kingsley Sanders; religious rites in
        Bali; a sermon to children in a Belfast church and a
        twist session; city of Leicester compared with the
        city of Nottingham.

G190   "Just Like the Ivy." Spectator, 28 May 1966, p. 691.

        Review of the theatrical production of A Heritage and
        Its History, by Julian Mitchell.

G191   "Just $10, Please, for My Mugger." Vogue, January
            1973, p. 112.

G192 "Key Personalities." Observer Weekend Review, 26
June 1966, p. 27.

Review of At the Piano, by Ivor Newton, and In Pursuit of Music, by Denis Matthews.

G193 "Kipling: A Celebration in Silence." Spectator, 24
November 1965, p. 833.

Review of The Art of Rudyard Kipling, by J. M. S.
Tompkins. Reprinted in Urgent Copy [D27].

G194 "Kipling and Kuch-nays." Spectator, 6 January 1967,
pp. 18-19.

Review of Kipling in India, by Louis L. Cornell, and
Rudyard Kipling, by J. I. M. Stewart. Reprinted in
Urgent Copy [D27].

G195 "Koestler's Danube." Spectator, 1 October 1965,
pp. 418-19.

Review of Thieves in the Night, The Gladiators, and
The Magi and the Commissar. Reprinted in Urgent
Copy [D27].

G196 "Lament for a Maker." Spectator, 8 January 1965,
p. 37.

T. S. Eliot made the minds who experienced his
poetry as well as the poetry itself.

G197 "Language as Movement." Encounter, 34 (January
1970), pp. 64-67.

Review of Changing English, by Simeon Potter, and
Tudor to Augustan English, by A. C. Partridge.

G198 "Language, Myth, and Mr. Updike." Commonweal,
11 February 1966, pp. 557-59.

See reply by John Updike [L120].

G199   "Late Tribute. " Spectator, 16 September 1966,
       p. 354.

       Review of Siegfried Sassoon: A Critical Study, by
       Michael Thorpe.

G200   "Lawful Ambitions. " Spectator, 26 March 1965,
       p. 391.

G201   "Leporine. " Listener, 11 July 1963, p. 66.

G202   "Let Your Son Be a Spy. " Punch, 15 May 1968,
       pp. 708-10.

G203   "Let's Have a Bloody Revolution. " Saturday Review,
       13 May 1978, p. 48.

G204   Letter. New York Times Magazine, 19 November
       1972, pp. 34, 118.

       A long, hot response to Anne H. McCormick's angry
       "Meeting New York Realistically" [L77], itself a re-
       sponse to Burgess's article on New York [G10].

G205   "Letter from England. " Hudson Review, 19 (Autumn
       1966), pp. 455-60.

G206   "Letter from England. " Hudson Review, 20 (Autumn
       1967), pp. 454-58.

G207   "Letter from Europe. " American Scholar, 36 (Spring
       1967), pp. 261-65.

G208   "Letter from Europe. " American Scholar, 38 (Spring
       1969), pp. 297-99.

G209   "Letter from Europe. " American Scholar, 38 (Autumn
       1969), pp. 684-86.

G210 "Letter from Europe." American Scholar, 39 (Summer 1970), pp. 502-04.

G211 "Letter from Europe." American Scholar, 40 (Winter 1970), pp. 119-22.

G212 "Letter from Europe." American Scholar, 40 (Summer 1971), pp. 514, 516, 518, 520.

G213 "Letter from Europe." American Scholar, 41 (Winter 1971-1972), pp. 139-42.

G214 "Letter from Europe." American Scholar, 41 (Summer 1972), pp. 425-28.

G215 "Letter from Europe." American Scholar, 42 (Winter 1972-1973), pp. 135-38.

G216 "Letter to a Tax Man." Guardian, 28 December 1966, p. 12.

G217 "Levitating a Little." Spectator, 3 February 1967, pp. 140-41.

Review of The Heat of the Sun, by Sean O'Faolain.

G218 "Lewis as Spaceman." Spectator, 20 May 1966, pp. 640-41.

Review of The Apes of God, by Wyndham Lewis. Reprinted in Urgent Copy [D27].

G219 "Lion's Roar." Library Journal, 1 February 1977, pp. 327-29.

G220 Listener, 12 November 1964, p. 769.

Review of My Life and Loves, by Frank Harris.

G221 Listener, 25 March 1965, p. 461.

Review of The Memoirs of a Malayan Official, by Victor Purcell.

G222 Listener, 23 December 1965, p. 1044.

Review of The Language of the Law, edited by Lois Blom-Cooper.

G223 "A Litre of Shandy." Guardian, 26 November 1965, p. 15.

G224 "A Little Threepenny-bit." Listener, 18 July 1963, pp. 104-05.

G225 "The Living Language: Novels Are Made of Words." Times Literary Supplement, 22 April 1965, p. 317.

G226 "London Letter." American Scholar, 36 (Autumn 1967), pp. 636-38.

G227 "London Letter." American Scholar, 37 (Spring 1968), pp. 312-15.

G228 "London Letter." American Scholar, 37 (Autumn 1968), pp. 647-49.

G229 "London Letter." Hudson Review, 20 (Spring 1967), pp. 99-104.

G230 "A Long Drink of Porter." Spectator, 31 January 1964, p. 151.

G231 "The Long Fountain Pen." Spectator, 17 June 1966, p. 764.

Review of Writer by Trade: A View of Arnold Bennett, by Dudley Barker.

G232 "Long Road to Nzima." Times Literary Supplement, 19 November 1976, p. 1443.

Review of A Supplement to the Oxford English Dictionary, Vol. 2, edited by R. W. Burchfield.

G233 "Looking for Centres." Listener, 22 August 1963, p. 286.

G234 "Lore and Disorder." Spectator, 18 April 1969, pp. 511-12.

Review of The British Folklorists: A History, by Richard M. Dorson.

G235 "Love and Sin in 1985. Excerpt from 1985." New York Times, 13 August 1978, pp. 271-72.

G236 "Love Story (19th Century Style)," New York Times, 27 April 1971, p. 43.

G237 "The Lower Depths." Guardian, 11 February 1966, p. 8.

G238 "Made in Heaven." Spectator, 9 April 1965, p. 476.

G239 "Making de White Boss Frown." Encounter, 27 (July 1966), pp. 54-58.

Review of Uncle Tom's Cabin, by Harriet Beecher Stowe, edited by John A. Woods. Reprinted in Urgent Copy [D27].

G240 "Le Mal Français: Is There a Reason for Being Cartesian?" New York Times Magazine, 29 May 1977, pp. 46-48, 52-53.

G241 "Man and Artist." Spectator, 25 November 1966, pp. 693-94.

Reviews of books about Dylan Thomas: Selected Letters of Dylan Thomas, edited by Constance Fitzgibbon; The Craft and Art of Dylan Thomas, by William T. Moynihan; A Garland for Dylan Thomas, by George J. Firmage and Oscar Williams. Reprinted in Urgent Copy [D27].

G242 "Man of Letters." Guardian, 23 April 1965, p. 9.

G243 "The Manicheans." Times Literary Supplement, 3 March 1966, pp. 153-54.

G244 "March." Listener, 5 September 1963, p. 360.

G245 "Master Beckett." Spectator, 21 July 1967, pp. 79-80.

Review of No's Knife, by Samuel Beckett, and Beckett at Sixty.

G246 "Matter of Manners." Guardian, 14 December 1966, p. 18.

G247 "Matters of Romance." Spectator, 23 September 1966, p. 384.

Review of Of Other Worlds: Essays and Stories, by C. S. Lewis, edited by Walter Hooper.

G248 "The Meaning of Meaning." Observer Weekend Review, 29 May 1966, p. 22.

Review of The Oxford Dictionary of English Etymology, edited by C. T. Onions.

G249 "A Metaphysical City." Listener, 4 July 1963, p. 30.

Weekly comments on BBC programs: includes reviews of documentaries on Berlin, a journey to a lumberjacking job, and a discussion by four professional women about contemporary romantic fiction.

G250 "MF (extract)." Times (London), 22 May 1971, p. 17.

G251 "Michelangelo: The Artist as Miracle Worker." Critic, 34, No. 3 (Spring 1976), pp. 12-22.

G252 "Mighty Lineless." Listener, 13 February 1964, pp. 286-87.

G253 "The Milton Revolution." Spectator, 28 April 1967, pp. 487-88.

Review of Milton: The Modern Phase, by Patrick Murray. Reprinted in Urgent Copy [D27].

G254 "Mirable Annals." Encounter, 34 (May 1970), pp. 65-68.

Review of The Literary Life, by Robert Phelps and Peter Deane.

G255 "The Modicum Is the Messuage." Spectator, 13 October 1967, p. 427.

Critique of McLuhanian thinking. Concludes that believing the medium is stronger than ideas is perhaps worse than believing that the message is all. Reprinted in Urgent Copy [D27].

G256 "Monarchy in Abeyance." Listener, 17 October 1963, p. 626.

G257 "More Comedians." Spectator, 21 April 1967, p. 454.

Review of May We Borrow Your Husband?, by Graham Greene.

G258 "Moses in a Lounge Suit." Spectator, 21 March 1970, pp. 374-75.

Review of the New English Bible, Oxford and Cambridge University Press.

G259 "Mulligan Stew: Irving Wallace Rewrites Ulysses." New York Times Book Review, 6 June 1971, pp. 5-6.

G260 "Multilingual." Observer Weekend Review, 6 December 1964, p. 28.

Review of The Mother Tongue, by Lancelot Hogben.

G261 "Murder Most Fair by Agatha the Good." Life, 1 December 1967, p. 8.

Review of Third Girl, by Agatha Christie.

G262 "Murray and His Monument." Times Literary Supplement, 30 September 1977, pp. 1094-95.

Review of Caught in the Web of Words: James Murray and the Oxford English Dictionary, by K. M. Elisabeth Murray. See letters in the Times Literary Supplement [L75], [L76] and responses from Frederick A. Pottle [L95] and Keith Walker [L122].

G263 "Music at the Millennium." HiFi, 26 (May 1976), pp. 46-49.

G264 "My Country 'Tis of Thee." Spectator, 23 February 1968, p. 228.

Burgess discusses patriotism, specifically his own attitude toward England.

G265 "My Dear Students." Letter. New York Times Magazine, 19 November 1972, pp. 20, 22, 30, 32.

Letter to his students at City College, New York: a
lecture and a plea for conservatism and standards of
excellence in a university education, including the
doubt that "one can run a scholarly course on one's
own thing." See response from Horace Porter [L94].

G266 "Mysteries." Spectator, 16 April 1965, p. 506.

G267 "Naked Mr. Gibbon." Spectator, 21 October 1966,
p. 521.

Review of Memoirs of My Life, by Edward Gibbon,
edited by Georges A. Bonnard.

G268 "Nerves in the Afternoon." Listener, 19 March 1964,
pp. 494-95.

G269 "New Fiction." Listener, 20 January 1966, p. 109.

Review of The Ghosts, by Kathryn Perutz: The Velvet
Bubble, by Alice Winter; There Goes Davey Cohen, by
Wendy Oliver; Last Exit to Brooklyn, by Hubert Selby,
Jr.; Love on the Dock, by Walter Greenwood; Snap-
shots: Towards a New Novel, by Alain Robbe-Grillet,
translated by Barbara Wright.

G270 "New Fiction." Listener, 3 February 1966, p. 181.

G271 "New Fiction." Listener, 17 February 1966, p. 253.

G272 "New Fiction." Listener, 3 March 1966, p. 325.

G273 "New Fiction." Listener, 7 April 1966, p. 515.

G274 "New Fiction." Listener, 21 April 1966, p. 589.

G275 "New Fiction." Listener, 5 May 1966, p. 659.

G276   "New Fiction." Listener, 19 May 1966, p. 733.

G277   "New Fiction." Listener, 14 July 1966, p. 65.

G278   "New Novels. " Listener, 24 March 1966, p. 445.

G279   "New Novels. " Listener, 16 June 1966, p. 883.

G280   "New Novels. " Listener, 30 June 1966, p. 955.

G281   "A New Turn on the Old Ferris Wheel. " Spectator,
        2 April 1965, p. 447.

        Review of The Destroyer, by Paul Ferris; Lunch with
        Ashurbanipal, by Wallace Hidick; Powdered Eggs, by
        Charles Simmons; Yes from No-Man's Land, by Ber-
        nard Kops.

G282   New York Times Book Review, 2 January 1972,
        pp. 1, 10-11.

        Review of My Life and Times, by Henry Miller. See
        response from Joseph Schrank [L104].

G283   "No Sense of Occasion. " Listener, 9 January 1964,
        p. 90.

G284   "Not So Gentle Craft. " Spectator, 12 March 1965,
        pp. 329-30.

G285   "Not So Plurabelle. " Listener, 1 August 1963,
        pp. 178-79.

G286   "Notes but Also Letters. " Guardian, 22 July 1966,
        p. 10.

G287   "Notes from the Blue Coast." Saturday Review, 15
        April 1976, p. 5.

G288   "Notes from the Blue Coast." Saturday Review, 28
        October 1978, p. 58.

G289   "Novel." New Encyclopaedia Britannica. 15th ed.
        Macropaedia, Vol. 13, 1978, pp. 276-99.

G290   "The Novel in 2000 A.D." New York Times Book
        Review, 29 March 1970, pp. 2, 19.

G291   "A Novelist's Sources Are Myth, Language and the
        Here-and-Now." New York Times Book Review,
        19 July 1964, pp. 5, 26.

        See response from Robert Umans [L118].

G292   "Now Thank We All...." Observer Review, 19 March
        1967, p. 27.

        Review of The Cambridge Hymnal, by David Holbrook
        and Elizabeth Poston.

G293   "Officers and Gentlemen." Listener, 14 September
        1967, pp. 340-41.

G294   "The Offshore Islanders." New York Times Book
        Review, 28 January 1973, p. 4.

        Review of England's People from Roman Occupation to
        the Present, by Paul Johnson.

G295   "On English in English." Spectator, 29 August 1966,
        pp. 233-34.

        Review of Essays by English and American Men of
        Letters, 1490-1839. Vol. I of The English Language,
        edited by W. F. Bolton. Reprinted in Urgent Copy
        [D27].

G296 "On Lengthy Matters." New York Times Book Review, 14 December 1975, p. 39.

Discusses the popularity of short novels that have trendy content.

G297 "On the End of Every Fork." Guardian, 20 November 1964, p. 9.

Review of The Naked Lunch, by William Burroughs.

G298 "On the Hopelessness of Turning Good Books into Films." New York Times, Arts and Leisure Section, 20 April 1975, pp. 1, 15.

See responses by Mike Montemore [L83], Warren Kronemeyer [L71], and Bernard Dick [L38].

G299 "The One and Only." Guardian, 17 April 1964, p. 8.

Review of A Singular Man, by J. P. Donleavy.

G300 "Open and Shut Case." Spectator, 10 March 1967, p. 281.

Review of The Turn of the Novel, by Alan Friedman.

G301 "Orwell's 1984." Times (London), 20 April 1977, p. 12.

See also the letter from William Alderson [L09] and the letter related to, but not really about, Burgess's article [L74].

G302 "Other Edens--Anthony's Eden." Punch, 12 April 1967, pp. 535-36.

G303 "Our Bedfellow, the Marquis de Sade." Horizon, 11 (Winter 1969), pp. 104-09.

G304 Our Sunday Visitor, 65 (May 1977), p. 2.

Tells of writing screenplay for television production Jesus of Nazareth; see also "The Gospel According to Anthony Burgess" [G133].

G305 "Pain." Listener, 20 February 1964, pp. 326-27.

G306 "The Panel Game." Letter. Times Literary Supplement, 3 November 1966, p. 1003.

G307 "Paperback Tiger." Spectator, 29 March 1968, p. 410.

Review of The Making of a Publisher, by Victor Weybright.

G308 "Parallel Spatial Matrix." Guardian, 15 April 1966, p. 9.

G309 "Partridge in a Word Tree." Encounter, 33 (July 1969), pp. 51-55.

Review of reissues of A Dictionary of Slang and Unconventional English from the Fifteenth Century to the Present Day and Shakespeare's Bawdy, by Eric Partridge.

G310 "Past Time and the River." Spectator, 5 February 1965, p. 176.

Review of Mallabee, by David Walker; Patterns of Three and Four, by Hubert Nicholson; Sheba's Landing, by Thomas Baird; The Cockpit, by Paul Bourquin; and The Hat of Authority, by John Sanders.

G311 "The Pattern and the Core." Spectator, 2 July 1965, pp. 20-21.

Review of three novels by Rose McCauley: Told by an Idiot, The Towers of Trebizond, and Pleasure of Ruins.

G312 "A Peck of Penny Wisdom." Guardian, 16 October
1964, p. 9.

Review of The Faber Book of Aphorisms, edited by
W. H. Auden and Louis Kronenberger.

G313 "Père et Fils." Listener, 8 August 1963, p. 214.

G314 "The Perfect Shavian." Spectator, 8 October 1965,
p. 452.

Review of Collected Letters of Bernard Shaw, edited
by Dan Lawrence. Reprinted in Urgent Copy [D27].

G315 "A Pilot for Our Pain." Guardian, 22 May 1964,
p. 6.

Review of The Diaries of Franz Kafka, edited by Max
Brod.

G316 "A Place for Nature." Listener, 30 May 1963,
pp. 938-39.

Weekly comments on BBC programs: reviews programs on nature, Dutch Guiana, excerpt of William
Golding's Lord of the Flies, a rough elegy about the
steam locomotive.

G317 "Places." New York Times Book Review, 8 April
1973, p. 28.

Review of Places, by James Morris.

G318 "Plastic Punks." Psychology Today, November 1977,
pp. 120, 122, 126.

G319 "Poet and Pedant." Spectator, 24 March 1967,
pp. 336-37.

Review of Speak, Memory, by Vladimir Nabokov. Reprinted in Urgent Copy [D27].

G320 "Poet from Parnassus." Spectator, 7 March 1969,
pp. 306-07.

Review of Poets through Their Letters, by Martin
Seymour-Smith.

G321 "Poetry for a Tiny Room." Yorkshire Post, 16 May
1963, p. 4. See also [L20.]

Review of Inside Mr. Enderby [A16] by Joseph Kell (a
pseudonym of Anthony Burgess), The Natural, by Bernard Malamud, and A Penny for the Guy, by Tio
Savory.

G322 "Politics in the Novels of Graham Greene." Journal
of Contemporary History, 2 (April 1967), pp. 93-99.

Reprinted in Urgent Copy [D27], as "The Greene and
the Red: Politics in the Novels of Graham Greene."

G323 "Politics of Graham Greene." New York Times Book
Review, 10 September 1967, pp. 2, 32, 34.

Reprinted in Page 2 [D23].

G324 "Polycarpic Polnay." Spectator, 11 December 1964,
pp. 820-21.

Review of The Plaster Bed, by Peter de Polnay; The
Night in Lisbon, by Erich Maria Remarque, translated
by Ralph Manheim; The Boy Who Wanted Peace, by
George Friel; and The Honey Bird, by Stuart Cloete.

G325 "Portrait of the Artist in Middle Age." Nation, 4
March 1968, pp. 309-10.

G326 "The Postwar American Novel: A View from the
Periphery." American Scholar, 35 (Winter 1965-
1966), pp. 150-56.

Reprinted in Urgent Copy [D27].

G327 "Powers That Be." Encounter, 24 (January 1965),
pp. 71-76.

Review of Corridors of Power, by C. P. Snow, and
Late Call, by Angus Wilson.

G328 "The Pride of Gormenghast." Spectator, 20 June
1970, pp. 819-20.

Review of A World Away, a memoir of Mervyn Peake
by Maeve Gilmore.

G329 "The Prince of Percussion." Times Literary Supplement, 10 June 1977, p. 706.

Review of Drum Roll, by James Blades.

G330 "The Pringles All Entire." Spectator, 5 November
1965, p. 591.

Review of Friends and Heroes, by Olivia Manning; A
Second Home, by Brian Glanville; Hurry Sundown, by
K. R. Gilden; Night of Camp David, by Fletcher
Knebel; The 38th Floor, by Clifford Irving; and The
Penetrators, by Anthony Gray.

G331 "Private Dialect of Husbands and Wives." Vogue,
June 1968, pp. 118-19.

G332 "Probing the Probers." Listener, 16 January 1964,
p. 128.

G333 "The Professional Viewpoint." Twentieth Century
Studies, 1 (November 1969), pp. 109-30.

Information by Burgess appears on pp. 110-11.

G334 "Prompt Book." Spectator, 15 December 1967,
pp. 751-52.

Review of The Oxford Companion to the Theatre, 3rd ed., edited by Phyllis Hartnoll.

G335 "Pronounced Vla-DEEM-ear Nah-BOAK-off." New York Times Book Review, 2 July 1967, pp. 1, 20.

G336 "Protestant Catholics." Punch, 6 March 1968, p. 357.

G337 "Pubbing and Dubbing in the Baaaaalmy 'Other England, '" Letter. New York Times, Travel and Leisure Sect., 25 February 1973, p. 4.

See Burgess's article "In the Other England ..." [G169] and Otto Janssen's response [L62].

G338 "Pukka Trumps and Lost Charpoys." Spectator, 12 April 1968, p. 499.

Review of Hobson-Jobson, by Henry Yule and H. C. Burnell.

G339 "The Purpose of Education." Spectator, 3 March 1967, p. 247.

Refers to his days of teaching in a state school and describes the personality of a good teacher.

G340 "Pushkin and Kinbote." Encounter, 24 (May 1965), pp. 74-78.

Review of Eugene Onegin, by Aleksandr Pushkin, translated by Vladimir Nabokov.

G341 "Quite a Piece of Amerenglish, Hopefully." Saturday Review, 2 September 1978, p. 50.

G342 "A Rap from Moscow." Listener, 6 February 1964, p. 246.

See also [G09].

G343   "Rare Plants under a Frosty Moon." Spectator, 8
       January 1965, p. 47.

       Review of The Multiple Modern God and Other Stories,
       by Stanley Berne, and Kaliyuga, by David Stacton.

G344   "Rationality in Drinks." Guardian, 23 November 1966,
       p. 16.

G345   "A Raven on the Aerial." Spectator, 6 May 1966,
       pp. 574-75.

       Review of Royal Foundation and Other Plays, by Simon
       Raven.

G346   "Reading Your Own." New York Times Book Review,
       4 June 1967, p. 6.

G347   "The Recovery of Mandelstam." Guardian, 7 January
       1966, p. 7.

G348   "Reflections on a General Election." Spectator, 20
       June 1970, pp. 812-13.

       Written from Malta. Describes himself as "an ideol-
       ogue or metaphysical man. As a Lancashire Catholic
       Jacobite I have to be a Tory."

G349   "Reflections on a Golden Ring." Listener, 28 Decem-
       ber 1967, pp. 838-39.

G350   "Required Reading." Spectator, 24 December 1965,
       pp. 846-47.

       Review of Fiction and the Reading Public, by Q. D.
       Leavis, and A Guide to English Literature, by F. W.
       Bateson.

G351   "The Reticence of Ulysses." Spectator, 7 June 1969,
       p. 748.

Relates censorship to writers' enjoyment of circum-
venting taboos. Observes that "post-Joyce freedom
may result in both literary sex and literary obscenity"
losing their effect through overuse. Written in Malta.

G352   "Return to Reality." Listener, 5 December 1963,
        p. 956.

G353   "Revers English." Intellectual Digest, 3 (April 1973),
        p. 58.

G354   "Romantic Ireland's Dead and Gone." Punch, 1 May
        1968, p. 651.

G355   "Rock of Ages." Guardian, 9 November 1966, p. 18.

G356   "Russian Roulette at 4:30 a.m." Listener, 9 May
        1968, pp. 614-15.

G357   "Sage and Mage of the Steam Age." Spectator, 15
        April 1966, p. 471.

        Review of Robert Browning: A Collection of Critical
        Essays, edited by Phillip Drew.

G358   "Said Mr. Cooper to His Wife: You Know, I Could
        Write Something Better Than That." New York
        Times Magazine, 7 May 1972, pp. 108, 112, 114-
        15.

G359   "Said Rudyard to Rider." Spectator, 29 October 1965,
        p. 550.

        Review of Rudyard Kipling to Rider Haggard: The
        Record of a Friendship, edited by Morton Cohen. Re-
        printed in Urgent Copy [D27].

G360   "Saying or Screaming Their Way." Guardian, 27
        November 1964, p. 15.

G361 "Science Fiction." <u>Observer Weekend Review</u>, 31 July
        1966, p. 21.

Review of Dune, by Frank Herbert; The Last Refuge,
by John Petty; All Fool's Day, by Edmund Cooper;
The Fury Out of Time, by Lloyd Biggle, Jr.; The
Menace from Earth, by Robert Heinlein; and SF6.

G362 "Seen Any Good Galsworthy Lately?" <u>New York Times</u>
        <u>Magazine</u>, 16 November 1969, pp. 57-59.

Discusses the television production of The Forsyte
Saga, by John Galsworthy. See also the response to
the article by David A. Kahn. [L65].

G363 "The Seventeenth Novel." <u>New York Times Book</u>
        <u>Review</u>, 21 August 1966, pp. 2, 14.

Expresses his fears, dissatisfactions, and doubts as
he writes a comic novel about a middle-aged poet
(Enderby Outside); fears repetitions of locales, situa-
tions, and the same kind of language; dissatisfied with
the restrictions of ordinary language and the forms
and rhythms of official or orthodox English; doubts
that authors set out to write experimental fiction, but
rather they experiment because they become bored.
Reprinted in Page 2 [D25].

G364 "Shakespeare in Music." <u>The Musical Times</u>, 105
        (December 1964), pp. 901-02.

Review of Shakespeare in Music: A Collection of
Essays, by John Stevens, Charles Cudworth, Winston
Dean, and Roger Fiske, with a Catalogue of Musical
Works, edited by Phyllis Hartnoll.

G365 "Shantih 3." <u>Listener</u>, 19 December 1963, pp. 1042-
        43.

G366 "Shem the Penman." <u>Spectator</u>, 2 December 1966,
        p. 726.

Review of Letters of James Joyce, Vols. II and III, edited by Richard Ellmann. Reprinted in Urgent Copy [D26].

G367 "Shrivel of Critics." Harper's, February 1977, pp. 87, 90-91.

G368 "Silence, Exile and Cunning." Listener, 6 May 1965, pp. 661-63.

G369 "Singapore Revisited." Spectator, 6 June 1970, p. 742.

Observations and comparisons, past and present, about Singapore, about which Burgess wrote in his first published novel, Time for a Tiger [A27].

G370 "Singer at the Feast." Guardian, 3 March 1967, p. 7.

G371 "Sins of Simony." Spectator, 15 October 1965, pp. 491-92.

Review of Friends in Low Places, by Simon Raven; The Egyptologists, by Kingsley Amis and Robert Conquest; Games of Chance, by Thomas Hinde; Sweet Morn of Judas' Day, by Richard Llewellyn; and A Suspension of Mercy, by Patricia Highsmith.

G372 "Sins of the State." Listener, 30 November 1967, pp. 730-31.

G373 "Sisters Under the Skin." Listener, 2 December 1965, p. 914.

Review of Talking to Women, by Nell Dunn.

G374 "Slangfest." Listener, 2 March 1967, p. 299.

G375 "Sleepbox." Listener, 25 January 1968, pp. 122-23.

G376 "Smooth Beawties." Spectator, 7 February 1970, pp. 179-80.

Review of The Works of Thomas Campion, edited by Walter R. Davis.

G377 "Sober City to Lift Your Heart." Daily Telegraph Magazine, 29 September 1972, p. 52.

G378 "Soft-Shelled Classics." Spectator, 10 February 1967, p. 171.

Review of paperback editions of classics.

G379 "Soil and Flower." Spectator, 28 October 1966, p. 554.

Review of The Novel and Society, by Diana Spearman.

G380 "Song in the Mist." Spectator, 9 December 1966, p. 762.

Review of The Early English and Celtic Lyric, by P. L. Henry.

G381 "Speaking of Writing." Times (London), 16 January 1964, p. 13.

G382 "Spectator Symposium." Spectator, 29 July 1966, p. 138.

Personal reflections of Britain's economic troubles and the threat of devaluation. Strongly criticizes Wilson's philosophy and socialism in general.

G383 "Spectator Symposium on 1967." Spectator, 6 January 1967, p. 6.

His hopes for the New Year.

G384   "Spectator Symposium on 1968." Spectator, 29 December 1967, p. 804.

Burgess's hopes for 1968.

G385   "Spring and Fall." Spectator, 30 April 1965, p. 563.

G386   "State Favoritism in Literature." Sunday Telegraph, 12 March 1968, p. 14.

G387   "The Steinerian Agony." Encounter, 29 (December 1967), pp. 79-82.

Review of Language and Silence, by George Steiner. Reprinted in Urgent Copy [D27].

G388   "The Story of the Weeper." Times Literary Supplement, 25 August 1978, p. 445.

Review of Magdalene, by Carolyn Slaughter.

G389   "Stryne Agyne." Listener, 31 March 1966, p. 480.

Review of Aussie English, by John O'Grady.

G390   "Summoned by Bell." Spectator, 9 June 1967, p. 682.

Review of Collected Poems 1937-1966, by Martin Bell.

G391   Sunday Times Magazine, 16 October 1977, p. 90.

Lists his own seven wonders of the world.

G392   "Surprise from the Grove." Observer Review, 3 September 1967, p. 22.

Review of The Third Policeman, by Flann O'Brien,
and Dubliners, by James Joyce.

G393 "Swing of the Censor." Spectator, 21 June 1969,
pp. 820-22.

More on censorship; history of certain books that were
accused of being pornographic. Written in Malta.

G394 "Symposia." Listener, 19 September 1963, pp. 440-
41.

G395 "Take a Wound, Take a Bow." Spectator, 5 March
1965, p. 305.

Review of A World Elsewhere, by John Bowen; The
Monkey Watches, by Robert Towers; Love from Venus
by Max Catto; The Satyr and the Saint, by Leonarto
Bercouici; and Across the Sea Wall, by Christopher
Koch.

G396 "Takeover." Listener, 23 May 1963, p. 884.

Weekly comments on BBC programs: Jorge Luis
Borges on his own work and his debt to English literature; Dino DeLaurentiis pushing on with his filming
of the whole Bible; reviews of shows on Mexico's Day
of the Dead, Iceland, Surinam, William Russo's para-
or meta-jazz, and an Elgar film.

G397 "Televalediction." Listener, 4 July 1968, pp. 27-28.

G398 "Television." Listener, 12 January 1967, p. 71.

G399 "Television." Listener, 9 February 1967, p. 207.

G400 "Television." Listener, 9 March 1967, p. 335.

G401 "Television." Listener, 6 April 1967, p. 471.

G402 "Television." Listener, 1 June 1967, p. 727.

G403 "Television." Listener, 29 June 1967, p. 863.

G404 "Television." Listener, 27 July 1967, p. 123.

G405 "Temporary Daughters." Listener, 12 September 1963, pp. 398-99.

G406 "Thanatos." Listener, 10 October 1963, pp. 582-83.

G407 "These Canapés Are Great!" Spectator, 24 November 1965, pp. 706-07.

Review of Winter Tales 11, edited by A. D. Maclean; Going to Meet the Man, by James Baldwin; The Smell of Bread, by Yury Kazakov; Stories, 1895-1897, by Anton Chekhov, edited by Ronald Hingley; Voices 2, by Michael Ratcliffe; The Wedding Party, by H. E. Bates; Collected Short Stories, by Robert Graves; The Hospitality of Miss Tolliver, by Gerald Kersh; Famous Tales of the Fantastic, edited by Herbert van Thal; and Great Short Stories of the World, edited by Whit Burnett and Hallie Burnett.

G408 "Think-Tank." Spectator, 3 May 1968, pp. 598-600.

Review of The Year 2000, by Herman Kahn and Anthony Weiner.

G409 "Thoughts of a Belated Father." Spectator, 6 September 1968, p. 322.

About his new stepson and their relationship--problems of communication and understanding.

G410 "Thoughts on the Thoughts." Spectator, 15 September 1967, p. 298.

Discusses Chairman Mao's Thoughts.

G411 "Three Sterling Islands: 1. The Rock." Listener,
29 December 1966, pp. 965-66.

G412 "Thundering Text." Listener, 20 June 1963, p. 1050.

Weekly comments on BBC programs: a week of
"thundering texts and sniveling commentaries," with a
favorable review of the new program "Tonight," whose
broadcasters never intimidate the viewers as do the
broadcasters of Panorama. "This has a good deal
to do with the various modifications of Received Stand-
ard English that most of them use--honest class or
regional phonemes that suggest the grammar rather
than the public school.

G413 "To Be or Not to Be in Love with You." Show,
(January 1970), pp. 75-80.

Discusses his script on the life of Shakespeare for
Warner Brothers. Includes excerpts from the script.
Working title: Bawdy Bard.

G414 "Together Again." Spectator, 29 September 1967,
pp. 363-65.

Review of The Company She Kept: Mary McCarthy,
Herself and Her Writing, by Doris Grumbach.

G415 "A Touch of Israel in Rome." Saturday Review, 29
April 1978, p. 45.

G416 "A Touch of the Apostasies." Spectator, 16 October
1964, p. 518.

G417 "A Trauma from the Fens." Spectator, 15 May 1964,
p. 667.

G418 "Travel 18th Century Style." Holiday, 42 (November
1967), pp. 72-77, 117, 128, 130.

G419 "Treasures and Fetters." Spectator, 21 February 1964, p. 254.

Reprinted in Urgent Copy [D27].

G420 "The Triple Thinker." Spectator, 14 January 1966, pp. 47-48.

Review of The Bit Between My Teeth: A Literary Chronicle of 1950-1965, by Edmund Wilson. Reprinted in Urgent Copy [D27].

G421 "The Trouble with Racine." Spectator, 2 April 1965, p. 442.

G422 "Troubled Bubbles." Spectator, 16 May 1969, p. 655.

Review of Secret Laughter, by Walter de la Mare.

G423 "The Truth of the True Shroud." Saturday Review, 25 November 1978, p. 12.

The mystery of the winding sheet in which Jesus's body was placed after crucifixion; the mythologizing of Christ's resurrection, which too often overshadows the important doctrines of charity and tolerance.

G424 "TV on TV." Listener, 12 December 1963, pp. 1000-01.

G425 "Twelve Hundred Pages and Four Marbles." Listener 2 June 1966, p. 804.

Review of Miss MacIntosh, My Darling, by Marguerite Young, and The Solid Mandala, by Patrick White.

G426 "A $200 Million Erector Set." New York Times Magazine, 23 January 1977, p. 14.

An article on the Beaubourg Center in Paris.

G427 "The Two Shaws." Spectator, 14 May 1965, pp. 635-
36.

Review of The Complete Plays of Bernard Shaw and
The Complete Prefaces of Bernard Shaw, by Paul Hamlyn. Reprinted in Urgent Copy [D27].

G428 "The Universal Mess." Guardian, 24 July 1964, p. 9.

Review of The Novels of Samuel Beckett, by John
Fletcher.

G429 "Vengeance as a Corruptor." Spectator, 30 April
1965, p. 575.

Review of Throw, by Anthony Bloomfield; Owe by Owen,
by Penelope Gilliatt; The Giant Dwarfs, by Gisela
Elsner, translated by Joel Carmichael; The Pond, by
Robert Murphy; and Nefertiti, by Nicole Vidal, translated by Johanna Harwood.

G430 "The Very Casques." Listener, 31 October 1963,
p. 712.

G431 "A Very Tragic Business." Spectator, 10 June 1966,
p. 731.

Review of Modern Tragedy, by Ramond Williams. Reprinted in Urgent Copy [D27].

G432 "Vieux Chapeau." New York Times Book Review,
3 March 1968, pp. 4-5.

G433 "Viewpoint." Times Literary Supplement, 21 April
1972, p. 446.

G434 "Viewpoint." Times Literary Supplement, 4 August
1972, p. 916.

G435 "Viewpoint. " Times Literary Supplement, 13 October 1972, p. 1224.

G436 "Viewpoint. " Times Literary Supplement, 1 December 1972, p. 1458.

G437 "Viewpoint. " Times Literary Supplement, 19 January 1973, p. 64.

Comments on New York, the Modern Language Association Convention, and television.

G438 "Viewpoint. " Times Literary Supplement, 23 March 1973, p. 322.

G439 "Viewpoint. " Times Literary Supplement, 11 May 1973, p. 526.

G440 "Viewpoint. " Times Literary Supplement, 22 June 1973, p. 718.

Views on the U.S. literary scene and his experience at Fordham University. See also letters by Leo Hamalian [L55], George W. Shea [L106], and Brian Stone [L111].

G441 "Viewpoint. " Times Literary Supplement, 24 August 1973, p. 976.

G442 "Views. " Listener, 31 August 1967, p. 261.

G443 "Views. " Listener, 7 March 1968, p. 295.

G444 "Views. " Listener, 14 November 1968, p. 634.

G445 "Views. " Listener, 22 May 1969, p. 709.

G446 "The Vocation of a Virtuoso." Times Literary Supplement, 8 April 1977, p. 419.

Review of Unfinished Journey, by Yehudi Menuhin. See response from Menuhin [L80].

G447 "Wagner's 'The Ring' ... A Number of Interpretations." Listener, 17 September 1964, pp. 419-21.

G448 "The Waste Land Revisited." Horizon, 14 (Winter 1972), pp. 104-09.

G449 "Watch Your Language." Observer Review (formerly titled The Observer Weekend Review), 15 January 1967, p. 26.

Review of The Treasure of Our Tongue, by Lincoln Barnett, and Personalities of Language, by Gary Jennings.

G450 "Waugh Begins." Encounter, 23 (December 1964), pp. 64, 66.

Review of A Little Learning: The First Volume of an Autobiography, by Evelyn Waugh. Reprinted in Urgent Copy [D27].

G451 "We Call This Friday Good." Spectator, 10 July 1964, pp. 59-60.

G452 "Weak, That Was." Listener, 3 October 1963, pp. 520-21.

G453 "The Wearing of the Greene." Guardian, 11 November 1966, p. 8.

G454 "The Weasels of Pop." Punch, 20 September 1967, pp. 430-31.

G455 "Whan That Aprille ... " Horizon, 13 (Spring 1971),
pp. 45-47, 57-59.

G456 "What a Sight It Were. " Listener, 30 April 1964,
pp. 730-31.

G457 "What Is Pornography?" Spectator, 1 December 1967,
pp. 683-84.

Discusses Last Exit to Brooklyn, by Hubert Selby,
Jr., and the recent decision of the courts on pornographic books. Reprinted in Perspectives on Pornography, edited by Douglas A. Hughes [D28], and in
Urgent Copy [D27].

G458 "What Now in the Novel?" Spectator, 26 March 1965,
p. 400.

Reprinted in Urgent Copy [D27].

G459 "What's All This Fuss About Libraries?" Library
Journal, 15 March 1968, pp. 1114-15.

Same as [G462].

G460 "What's Going On There. " Guardian, 27 January 1967,
p. 7.

G461 "Where Is English?" New Society, 21 July 1966,
pp. 100-01

G462 "Why All This Fuss About Libraries?" Spectator,
3 November 1967, p. 529.

Presents arguments against great libraries. Reprinted
in Library Journal [G459] and in Urgent Copy [D27].

G463 "Why, This Is Hell. " Listener, 1 October 1964,
p. 514.

G464 "The Wide-Eyed View." Guardian, 25 November 1966, p. 14.

Review of The Mind of the European Romantics, by H. G. Schenk.

G465 "Woman and Women: American Woman Is the Eternal Temptress." Vogue, 1 October 1969, pp. 194, 262-63.

G466 "Word, World and Meaning." Times Literary Supplement, 6 May 1965, p. 350.

Reprinted in Urgent Copy [D27].

G467 "Work and Play." New York Times Book Review, 5 June 1966, p. 1.

G468 "The Writer and Music." Listener, 3 May 1962, pp. 761-62.

Reviewing novels on the great romantic composer, Burgess finds none but Thomas Mann's Dr. Faustus to have created a credible composer; the jazz pianist in John Wain's Strike the Father Dead is unconvincing. Notes that the novelist has much to learn from musical form but should know where literature ends and music begins. Refers to his own experience as a jazz pianist.

G469 "The Writer as Drunk." Spectator, 4 November 1966, p. 588.

Review of Brendan Behan, Man and Showman, by Rae Jeffs. Reprinted in Urgent Copy [D27].

G470 "Writer's Pay." Listener, 3 December 1964, p. 896.

G471 "The Writer's Purpose." New York Times Book Review, 1 May 1966, p. 2.

G472 "Writing in Rome." Times Literary Supplement, 31
      October 1975, p. 1296.

      Discusses Italian writers with detailed comments on
      the poet Belli and his own translations of Belli's
      poems. See responses by J. M. Edelstein [L41] and
      Edwin Morgan [L84].

G473 "W. Somerset Maugham: 1874-1965." Listener,
      23 December 1965, p. 1033.

G474 "Yards and Yards of Entrails." Observer Weekend
      Review, 13 February 1966, p. 27.

      Review of Nova Express, by William Burroughs.

G475 "Yin and Bitters." Guardian, 18 November 1966,
      p. 7.

      Review of Don't Never Forget, by Brigid Brophy.

G476 Yorkshire Post, 16 May 1963, p. 4.

      Review of Inside Mr. Enderby, by Joseph Kell (a
      pseudonym of Anthony Burgess). See [A16].

G477 "Yuleovision." Listener, 2 January 1964, pp. 34-35.

H. INTERVIEWS

H01   Bunting, Charles T. "An Interview in New York with
       Anthony Burgess. " Studies in the Novel, 5 (Winter
       1973), pp. 505-29.

An interview with Burgess while he was serving as
Distinguished Professor of English at the City College.
Includes: (1) Burgess's writing plans: wants to write
a novel about a composer, a novel about Napoleon, and
a novel about the Papacy; (2) other writers and their
works: Shakespeare, Thomas Pynchon (perhaps "America's best living novelist"), A. L. Rowse, Leslie Hotson, James Joyce, George Orwell, Hannah Arendt,
B. S. Johnson, Michel Butor, Nathalie Sarrute, B. F.
Skinner (describes Beyond Freedom and Dignity as
"one of the most dangerous books ever written"), David
Karp, Graham Greene, Frank Kermode (England's best
scholar and critic, the only sensible critic in England
of Burgess's works), Pearl Buck, Vladimir Nabokov,
and John Updike; (3) Burgess's own works: series on
the life of Moses for Italian television, translation of
Cyrano de Bergerac, Napoleon Symphony, A Vision of
Battlements, Shakespeare, Nothing Like the Sun, A
Clockwork Orange, The Wanting Seed, One Hand Clapping ("I tried becoming a woman" for this novel with
a female protagonist; "not too difficult, really. "), The
Long Day Wanes, Tremor of Intent, The Eve of Saint
Venus, and Enderby (written in 1959, but not published
until 1963 "because the publishers thought it was un-
gentlemanly to write a book about a man sitting in the
lavatory all the time. "); (4) general comments on New
York, woman, theology in his novels.

H02   Churchill, Thomas. "An Interview with Anthony Bur-
       gess. " Malahat Review, No. 17 (January 1971),
       pp. 103-27.

An interview with Burgess at his Chiswick flat before
he left England. Includes: (1) Burgess's approach to
writing: claims not to be a great worker but an
energetic and consistent worker, staying "at the table
for a long stretch, smoking a lot," working "every
day, including weekends"; (2) Burgess's writing plans:
wants to write a novel about Manchester, a novel that
will be "the first of the structuralist novels ... based
on the Levi-Strauss theatre of the correlation between
language and social forms" (appeared as MF), a novel
of Joyce's life, and a work about a composer; (3) the
problem of using the pseudonym "Joseph Kell": creat-
ing a new author "means you have to start promoting
a new author"; (4) other writers and their works:
John Barth, Saul Bellow, John Braine, Ken Kesey,
Philip Roth, James Joyce, Vladimir Nabokov, Hubert
Selby, Jr., Anthony Powell, Keith Waterhouse, William Styron, Allan Sillitoe, and Evelyn Waugh; (5)
Burgess's own works: A Clockwork Orange, Enderby,
Nothing Like the Sun ("The book itself is a fake in
that it is enclosed in a [drunken final] lecture" given
by a man (Burgess himself) to "some Malayan students."), A Vision of Battlements ("a self-portrait"),
and The Wanting Seed.

H03   Clemons, Walter. "Anthony Burgess: Pushing On."
        New York Times Book Review, 29 November 1970,
        p. 2.

H04   Cullinan, John. "The Art of Fiction XLVIII: Anthony
        Burgess." Paris Review, 14, No. 56 (Spring
        1973), pp. 119-63.

An interview conducted through an exchange of letters
and a tape recording session at the University of
Wisconsin, during the time Burgess was serving as
Distinguished Professor of English at the City College
of New York. Includes: (1) the question of over-
production: "It has been a sin to be prolific only
since the Bloomsbury group--particularly (E. M.)
Forster--made it a point of good manners to produce,
as it were, costively. I've been annoyed less by
sneers at my alleged over-production than by the im-
putation that to write much means to write badly....
I've just put in rather more hours a day at the task

than some writers seem able to. "; (2) a description
of the ideal reader of Burgess as "a lapsed Catholic
and failed musician, short-sighted, color-blind, audi-
torily biased, who has read the books that I have
read" and is about Burgess's age; (3) Burgess's writing plans: preparing stage translations, possibly re-
turning to music, and working on a novel "to express
the feel of England in Edward III's time, using Dos
Passos' devices"; (4) other writers and their works:
Evelyn Waugh, Thomas Mann, Vladimir Nabokov, T.
S. Eliot, James Joyce, Edmond Rostand, John Dos
Passos, Mary Renault, Ford Madox Ford, Graham
Greene, F. Scott Fitzgerald, Ernest Hemingway, J.
D. Salinger, Daniel Defoe, Henry Fielding, Lawrence
Durrell, and Georges Simenon; (5) Burgess's own works:
Joysprick ("halfway between literary criticism and
linguistics"), It Is the Miller's Daughter (his one un-
finished novel, unfinished because "the sight of the
extract in cold print (in the Transatlantic Review,
[B03] turned me against the project"), Enderby, Cyrano
de Bergerac translation and adaptation for the stage,
A Vision of Battlements, A Clockwork Orange (doesn't
like having two different versions, British and American, of the book), Tremor of Intent, and Honey for
the Bears; (6) Manicheeism, the notion of essential
opposition, and his works; (7) and politics ("The U.
S. Presidency is a Tudor monarchy plus telephones. ").

H05   Dix, Carol. "Anthony Burgess. " Transatlantic Re-
      view, pp. 42-43 (Spring-Summer 1972), pp. 183-91.

H06   _____. "The Mugging Machine. " Guardian, 1
      January 1972, p. 8.

An interview article with Burgess while he was in
England for a preview screening of Stanley Kubrick's
film A Clockwork Orange. Includes Burgess's re-
collections of the writing of the novel on which the
film is based, his views of British society in 1961,
when he was writing the novel, and his comments on
Nadsat; criticizes the heavy-handed censorship in
Malta, where he moved after leaving England; notes
that he would like to write a musical.

H07   Edelhart, Mike. "More Fiction Writing Tips."
       Writer's Digest, August 1975, p. 13.

       Explains that short fiction does not allow the writer to
       develop characters or situations adequately; notes that
       short fiction is not marketable, while novels are; re-
       commends that young writers open a dictionary, let
       the words on the randomly selected page suggest a
       description of a room, a person, or a setting.

H08   Ehrlich, A. W. "Anthony Burgess: The Author of
       A Clockwork Orange Now Switches His Attention to
       Napoleon's Stomach." Publishers Weekly, 31 Jan-
       uary 1972, pp. 182-83.

H09   The Firing Line. Interviewed by William F. Buckley.
       Public Broadcasting System. 31 December 1972.

H10   Hicks, Jim. "Eclectic Author of His Own Five Foot
       Shelf." Life, 25 October 1968, pp. 87-97.

       An important early interview conducted shortly before
       the publication of Urgent Copy [D27] and before Bur-
       gess left England for Malta. Includes: (1) his crit-
       icism of critics who claim that he has written care-
       lessly because he has written so many books; (2)
       explains why he used the pseudonym "Joseph Kell,"
       and how he happened to write a review of a Joseph
       Kell novel [A16]; (3) relates the story of how he mis-
       takenly applied for a teaching job in Malaya instead of
       on the Island of Sark.

H11   Horder, John. "Art That Pays." Guardian, 10
       October 1964, p. 5.

H12   Krebs, Albin. "Notes on People." New York Times,
       11 April 1974, p. 47.

H13   Lewis, Anthony. "I Love England, but I Will No
       Longer Live There." New York Times Magazine,
       3 November 1968, pp. 38-40, 44, 47, 49, 52, 54,
       57-62, 64.

An introductory article and key early interview, in which Burgess discusses how he became a novelist and the faults of England, politics, and culture.

H14   Malko, George. Penthouse, 3, No. 10 (American edition), June 1972, p. 82.

H15   Morley, Sheldon. "Anthony Burgess Answers Back." Times (London), 6 August 1973, p. 7.

H16   "Playboy Interview: Anthony Burgess." Playboy, September 1974, pp. 69-70, 72, 74-76, 78, 80, 82, 84, 86.

H17   Pritchard, K. "A Candid Interview with the Author of A Clockwork Orange." Seventeen, August 1973, pp. 236, 249-50.

H18   Reilly, Lemuel. "An Interview with Anthony Burgess." Delaware Literary Review (University of Delaware), 2 (1973), pp. 48-55.

H19   Riemer, G. National Elementary Principal, 50, No. 6 (May 1971), pp. 9-21.

H20   Robinson, Robert. "On Being a Lancashire Catholic." Listener, 30 September 1976, pp. 397, 399.

I. RECORDINGS

I01   Anthony Burgess Reads from A Clockwork Orange and Enderby. Spoken Arts, SA 1120, 1974.

I02   Anthony Burgess Reads from The Eve of St. Venus and Nothing Like the Sun. Caedmon, TC 1442, 1974.

Recorded June 4, 1974. Notes by E. P. Swenson on the slipcase.

I03   A Clockwork Orange. Recorded by Anthony Burgess. Caedmon, TC 1417, 1973.

Notes by Burgess and M. Mantell on the slipcase. Includes chapters 1, 2, and 4.

Works About

Anthony Burgess

J. BOOKS, SECTIONS OF BOOKS

J01   Bergonzi, Bernard. "Anthony Burgess." In Contemporary Novelists. Ed. James Vinson. New York:
St. Martin's, 1972, pp. 202-06.

J02   _____. The Situation of the Novel. London: Macmillan, 1970, passim. Pittsburgh: University of
Pittsburgh Press, 1971. Claims that A Clockwork
Orange [A04] and The Wanting Seed [A30] are Burgess's finest novels, The Right to an Answer [A26]
one of his funniest and Nothing Like the Sun [A24]
his "triumph of stylistic invention and historical
re-creation." Concludes that "Burgess's peculiar
and challenging value is that he speaks, urbanely
enough, the same language as our dominant literary
and intellectual culture, but rejects many of its
basic, unexamined assumptions."

J03   Contemporary Authors: A Biobibliographical Guide to
Current Authors and Their Works. Vol. 1-4.
Detroit: Gale Research, 1962, pp. 136-37.

J04   Current Biography, 33 (May 1972), pp. 11-13.

J05   Current Biography Yearbook 1972. New York: Wilson,
1973, pp. 54-57.

J06   DeVitis, A. A. Anthony Burgess. Twayne's English
Authors Series. Ed. Sylvia E. Bowman. New
York: Twayne, 1972.

125

J07   Dix, Carol M. Anthony Burgess. Writers and Their
       Work. Ed. Ian Scott-Kilvert. London: Longman,
       for the British Council, 1971.

J08   Elsaesser, Thomas. "Screen Violence: Emotional
       Structure and Ideological Function in A Clockwork
       Orange. " In Approaches to Popular Culture. Ed.
       C. W. E. Bigsby. London: Arnold, 1976. Bowl-
       ing Green, Ohio: Popular, 1976, pp. 171-200.

J09   Engelborghs, Maurits. "Romans van een Woordkun-
       stenaar" (Novels by an Artist in Words). Dietsche
       Warande en Belfort (Antwerp), No. 1, pp. 59-62.

J10   Enright, D. J. "A Modern Disease: Anthony Bur-
       gess's Shakespeare. " In his Man Is an Onion:
       Reviews and Essays. LaSalle, Ill. : Library Press,
       1973, pp. 39-43. Same as "Mr. W. S. , " a review
       of Nothing Like the Sun [A24].

J11   Friedman, Melvin J. The Vision Obscured: Percep-
       tions of Some Twentieth-Century Catholic Novelists.
       New York: Fordham University Press, 1970,
       pp. 1, 6, 7-10.

J12   Grigson, Geoffrey. "On Collecting One's Reviews. "
       In his The Contrary View: Glimpses of Fudge and
       Gold. Totowa, N. J. : Rowman and Littlefield,
       1974, pp. 102-04. Same as "Insatiable Liking, " a
       review of Urgent Copy [D27].

J13   Hoffman, Charles G. , and A. C. Hoffman. "Mr. Kell
       and Mr. Burgess: Inside and Outside Mr. Enderby."
       In The Shaken Realist: Essays in Modern Literature
       in Honor of Frederick J. Hoffman. Ed. Melvin J.
       Friedman and John B. Vickery. Baton Rouge:
       Louisiana State University Press, 1970, pp. 300-10.
       "The two strands of Burgess's art, the comic and
       the tragic, become one vision in the Enderby novels,
       a black comedy of the contemporary scene. " Also
       notes Burgess's sharp eye for the ridiculous in

in human nature and his sharp ear for nuances in speech.

J14   Hyman, Stanley. "Anthony Burgess." In On Contemporary Literature: An Anthology of Critical Essays on the Major Movements and Writers of Contemporary Literature. Ed. Richard Kostelanetz. New York: Avon, 1964, pp. 300-05. New York: Avon, 1969, pp. 300-05. Expanded edition. Describes Burgess as an able satirist in the vein of Evelyn Waugh. Observes that Burgess's "grotesque surrealism" runs through The Right to an Answer [A26], Devil of a State [A08], A Clockwork Orange [A04], and The Wanting Seed [A30]. Comments on Burgess's use of and obsession with language, the Nadsat language of A Clockwork Orange, and his vocabulary in The Wanting Seed.

J15   The International Authors and Writers Who's Who. 8th ed. Ed. Brian Gaster. Cambridge, Eng.: International Bibliographical Centre, 1977, p. 143.

J16   International Who's Who, 1978-79. 42nd ed. London: Europa, 1978, p. 242.

J17   Irwin, W. R. The Game of the Impossible: A Rhetoric of Fantasy. Urbana: University of Illinois Press, 1976, pp. x, 59, 80, 190, 192-94.

J18   Ivask, Ivar, and Gero von Wilpert. World Literature Since 1945: Critical Surveys of the Contemporary Literatures of Europe and the Americas. New York: Frederick Ungar, 1973, p. 116.

J19   Johnson, Joseph J. "Anthony Burgess, MF," In Literary Annual. New York: Salem, 1972, pp. 223-25.

J20   Karl, Frederick R. A Reader's Guide to the Contemporary English Novel. Rev. ed. New York: Farrar, Straus and Giroux, 1972, pp. 327, 355, 360-3.

J21   Kennard, J. E. "Anthony Burgess: Double Vision."
        In Numbers and Nightmares: Forms and Fantasies
        in Contemporary Fiction. Hamden, Conn.: Archon,
        1975, pp. 131-54.

J22   Lodge, David. The Novelist at the Crossroads and
        Other Essays on Fiction and Criticism. Ithaca,
        N. Y.: Cornell University Press, 1971, pp. 19-21.

J23   Morris, Robert K. "Anthony Burgess, The Malayan
        Trilogy: The Futility of History." In his Continu-
        ance and Change. Crosscurrents/Modern Critiques.
        Ed. Harry T. Moore. Carbondale: Southern Il-
        linois University Press, 1972, pp. 71-92.

J24   _____. The Consolations of Ambiguity: An Essay
        on the Novels of Anthony Burgess. Literary Fron-
        tiers Edition. Columbia: University of Missouri
        Press, 1971.

J25   Page, Norman. Speech in the English Novel. Lon-
        don: Longmans, 1973. Only one reference, on
        p. 9, to The Doctor Is Sick [A09].

J26   Rabinovitz, Rubin. The Reaction Against Experiment
        in the English Novel, 1950-1960. New York:
        Columbia University Press, 1967.

J27   Schoenbaum, S. "Burgess and Gibson." In his
        Shakespeare's Lives. Oxford: Clarendon Press,
        1970, pp. 765-68.

J28   Seymour-Smith, Martin. Who's Who in Twentieth
        Century Literature. New York: Holt, Rinehart
        and Winston, 1976, pp. 61-62.

J29   Scholes, Robert. Structural Fabulation: An Essay

on Fiction of the Future. Ward-Phillips Lectures in English Language and Literature, Vol. 7. Notre Dame, Ind.: University of Notre Dame Press, 1975, pp. 23, 71, 79.

J30   Solotaroff, Theodore. "The Busy Hand of Burgess." In his The Red Hot Vacuum, and Other Pieces on the Writing of the Sixties. New York: Atheneum, 1970, pp. 269-75.

J31   Stone, Donald David. Novels in a Changing World: Meredith, James and the Transformation of English Fiction in the 1880's. Cambridge, Mass.: Harvard University Press, 1972. One mention of Burgess on p. 336: "At the present time, Anthony Burgess seems the most Meredithian of novelists in terms of his prodigious literary gifts and his curious use of them."

J32   Tilton, John W. "A Clockwork Orange: Awareness Is All." Chapter 2 in his Cosmic Satire in the Contemporary Novel. Lewisburg, Pa.: Bucknell University Press, 1977, pp. 21-42.

J33   Tufte, Virginia. Grammar as Style. New York: Holt, Rinehart and Winston, 1971, pp. 13, 79, 130, 190. Includes examples from Burgess's works, Enderby [A10] and The Novel Now [D19].

J34   200 Contemporary Authors. Ed. Barbara Harte and Carolyn Riley. Detroit: Gale Research, 1969, p. 60.

J35   Ward, A. C. Longman Companion to Twentieth Century Literature. London: Longmans, 1970, pp. 98-99.

J36   Who's Who, 1970-71.

J37   Who's Who, World, 1971.

K. DISSERTATIONS

K01   Arnold, Voiza Olson. "Narrative Structure and the
      Readers Theatre Staging of Nothing Like the Sun by
      Anthony Burgess." University of Illinois at Urbana-
      Champaign, 1975.

K02   Brown, Rexford Glenn. "Conflict and Confluence:
      The Art of Anthony Burgess." University of Iowa,
      1971.

K03   Cullinan, John Thomas. "Anthony Burgess' Novels:
      A Critical Introduction." Columbia University,
      1972.

K04   Holte, Carlton Thomas. "Taming the Rock: Myth,
      Model and Metaphor in the Novels of Anthony Bur-
      gess." University of California at Davis, 1978.

K05   Mablekos, Carole Marbes. "The Artist as Hero in
      the Novels of Joyce Cary, Lawrence Durrell, and
      Anthony Burgess." Purdue University, 1974.

K06   Moran, Kathryn Lou. "Utopias, Subtopias, Dystopias
      in the Novels of Anthony Burgess." University of
      Notre Dame, 1974.

K07   Siciliano, Sam Joseph. "The Fictional Universe of
      Four Science Fiction Novels: Anthony Burgess's
      A Clockwork Orange, Ursula Le Guin's The Word
      for World Is Forest, Walter Miller's A Canticle

for Leibowitz and Roger Zelazny's Creatures of
Light and Darkness. " University of Iowa, 1975.

K08   Stinson, John Jerome. "The Uses of the Grotesque
       and Other Modes of Distortion: Philosophy and
       Implication in the Novels of Iris Murdoch, William
       Golding, Anthony Burgess, and J. P. Donleavy."
       New York University, 1971.

K09   Wagner, Kenyon Lewis. "Anthony Burgess's Mytho-
       poeic Imagination: A Study of Selected Novels
       (1956-1968)." Texas Tech University, 1974.

L. ARTICLES AND ESSAYS

L01   Adler, Dick. "Inside Mr. Burgess." Sunday Times
      Magazine, 2 April 1967, pp. 47-50.

L02   Aggeler, Geoffrey. "Between God and Notgod: An-
      thony Burgess' Tremor of Intent." Malahat Review,
      No. 17 (January 1971), pp. 90-102.

L03   _____. "The Comic Art of Anthony Burgess."
      Arizona Quarterly, 25 (Autumn 1969), pp. 234-51.
      Describes Burgess, who had written seventeen
      novels in the preceding twelve years, as "one of
      the most versatile and prolific present masters of
      black comedy." Notes that his works are linguistic
      feats as well as literary accomplishments, although
      "even the most enthusiastic admirer of Burgess's
      novels must admit that he has not yet produced a
      truly great comic novel."

L04   _____. "Incest and the Artist: Anthony Burgess's
      MF as Summation." Modern Fiction Studies, 18
      (Winter 1972-1973), pp. 529-43.

L05   _____. "Mr. Enderby and Mr. Burgess." Malahat
      Review, No. 10 (April 1969), pp. 104-110.

L06   _____. "Pelagius and Augustine in the Novels of
      Anthony Burgess." English Studies, 55 (February
      1974), pp. 43-55.

L07   _____. "A Prophetic Acrostic in Anthony Burgess's

132

Nothing Like the Sun. " Notes and Queries, N. S. 21 (Vol. 219 in continuous series) (April 1974), p. 136. See also Burgess's article "Genesis and Headache" [D05] for comments on this subject.

L08 _____ . "A Wagnerian Affirmation: Anthony Burgess's The Worm and the Ring. " Western Humanities Review, 27 (1973), pp. 401-10.

L09 Alderman, William. "Orwell's 1984. " Letter. Times (London), 2 May 1977, p. 13. Response to Burgess's critique of 1984 [G301].

L10 Anderson, Ken. "A Note on A Clockwork Orange. " Notes on Contemporary Literature, 2 (November 1972), pp. 5-7. Comments on the meanings and connotations of "orange" in British colloquial speech. See also Burgess's article, "Clockwork Marmalade" [G60], for an explanation of the source and meaning of the phrase "clockwork orange. "

L11 "Anthony Burgess. " National Observer, 27 April 1970, p. 19.

L12 "Author Tries Hand at Book-Selling. " New York Times, 2 June 1973, p. 18. Concerns Burgess's attempt to sell his translation and adaptation of Cyrano de Bergerac without a publisher.

L13 "ATV in 6 Million Pound European Co-Production Venture, " Times (London), 19 December 1972, p. 5. Announces that Burgess and Vittoria Bonicelli will write the script for Moses, to be presented in a series of one-hour dramas.

L14 Bentley, Nicholas. "Ugh. " Letter. Times Literary Supplement, 16 January 1964, p. 53. Response to Burgess's "In Defense of William Burroughs" [G167].

L15 Berlins, Marcel. "Lawyers Reject Author's Attack. "

Times (London), 7 August 1973, p. 2. Immediate reaction in legal circles to Burgess's criticism of judges' vague attacks on and condemnation of the film A Clockwork Orange, which was based on his book. Claims that Burgess's criticism aimed at the wrong persons.

L16   Betts, Ernest. "Millions on a Musical About Shakespeare." Times (London), 24 August 1968, p. 18. Report on Burgess's script and musical score for a film about Shakespeare's life.

L17   Brooke-Rose, Christine. "Le Roman Experimental en Angleterre." Les Langues Moderne, 63, No. 2 (March-April 1969), pp. 158-68.

L18   Brophy, Elizabeth. "A Clockwork Orange: English and Nadsat." Notes on Contemporary Literature, 2, No. 2 (March 1972), pp. 4-6.

L19   Brown, Les. "NBC Buys an Anglo-Italian Series on the Life of Jesus." New York Times, 1 August 1974, p. 57.

L20   "Burgess and--Kell." Yorkshire Post, 20 May 1963. An editorial disclaimer of Burgess's review of Inside Mr. Enderby [A16], by Joseph Kell, a pseudonym of Burgess. See also [G321].

L21   "Burgess to Write Script for 'Moses.'" New York Times, Arts Section, 30 January 1973, p. 25. Burgess to write the script for an Italian-British television production starring Burt Lancaster.

L22   Byrne, K. "There Is No Place for Home." Maclean's, 6 November 1978, p. 62.

L23   Carson, Julie. "Pronominalization in A Clockwork Orange." Papers on Language and Literature, 12

(1976), pp. 200-05. Analyzes Alex's systematic use
of the pronominal forms "thou" and "you. "

L24 Cartey, Wilfred. "The Dawn, The Totem, The
Drums. " Commonweal, 12 May 1967, pp. 227-30.

L25 Carvalho, Alredo Leme Coelho de. "As distopias de
Anthony Burgess. " Revista de Letros de Faculdade
de Filsofia, Ciencias, e Letros de Assis, 15 (1973),
pp. 9-34.

L26 Chew, Shirley. "Mr. Livedog's Day: The Novels of
Anthony Burgess. " Encounter, 38 (June 1972),
pp. 57-64.

L27 Citrin, Marion. "Not for Reading. " Letter. New
York Times Book Review, 1 January 1967, p. 21.
Reply to Burgess's article "The Book Is Not for
Reading" [G47].

L28 Cleworth, Joan. "Charlotte, Not Emily. " Letter.
New York Times, 1 April 1973, p. 36. Reply to
Burgess's "Boo" [G46].

L29 Connelly, Wayne C. "Optimism in Burgess's A Clockwork Orange. " Extrapolation: A Journal of Science
Fiction and Fantasy, 14, No. 1 (December 1972),
pp. 25-29.

L30 Corcoran, Neil. "Anthony Burgess's Viewpoint. "
Letter. Times Literary Supplement, 30 March
1973, p. 353. Response to Burgess's 23 March
1973 "Viewpoint" [G438].

L31 Cullinan, John. "Anthony Burgess' A Clockwork
Orange: Two Versions. " English Language Notes,
9 (June 1972), pp. 287-92.

L32   Cullinan, John. "Burgess' The Wanting Seed." Ex-
       plicator, 31, No. 7 (March 1973), item 51.

L33   Cullinan, John. "Anthony Burgess' 'The Muse: A
       Sort of SF Story.'" Studies in Short Fiction, 9
       (1972), pp. 213-20.

L34   Dahlie, Hallvard. "Brian Moore: An Interview."
       Tamarack Review, 46 (Winter 1968), pp. 7-29.
       Reference to Burgess on p. 23.

L35   Damant, David. "Ugh." Letter. Times Literary
       Supplement, 9 January 1964, p. 27. Response to
       Burgess's "In Defense of William Burroughs"
       [G167].

L36   Davis, Earle. "Laugh Now--Think Later! The Genius
       of Anthony Burgess." Kansas Magazine, (1968),
       pp. 7-12.

L37   Derrick, Christopher. "This Our Exile: The Novels
       of Anthony Burgess." Triumph, 2 (February 1967),
       pp. 28-30, 32-33.

L38   Dick, Bernard F. "Who Said Good Books Make Bad
       Movies?" Letter. New York Times, 18 May
       1975, Sect. 2, p. 19. Reply to Burgess's article
       "On the Hopelessness of Turning Good Books into
       Films" [G298].

L39   Dimeo, Steven. "The Ticking of an Orange." River-
       side Quarterly, 5 (1973), pp. 318-21. Compares
       Burgess's novel A Clockwork Orange [A04] to Stan-
       ley Kubrick's film [A05].

L40   Donley, Michael. "Translation." Letter. Times
       Literary Supplement, 25 September 1970, pp. 1094-
       95. Reply to Burgess's "Bless Thee Bottom ..."
       [G42].

L41   Edelstein, J. M. "Writing in Rome." Letter. Times
       Literary Supplement, 21 November 1975, p. 1388.
       Response to Burgess's "Writing in Rome" [G471].

L42   Evans, Robert O. "Nadsat: The Argot and Its Im-
       plications in Anthony Burgess' A Clockwork Orange."
       Journal of Modern Literature, 1 (1971), pp. 406-10.

L43   Evans, Robert O. "The Nouveau Roman, Russian
       Dystopias, and Anthony Burgess." Studies in the
       Literary Imagination, 6, No. 2 (Fall 1973), pp. 27-
       37.

L44   Fernando, Lloyd. "Literary English in the South-East
       Asian Tradition. Westerly, No. 3 (September 1971),
       pp. 7-13.

L45   Fiore, Peter Amadeus. "Milton and Kubrick: Eden's
       Apple or a Clockwork Orange." CEA Critic, 35,
       No. 2 (January 1973), pp. 14-17.

L46   Fitzpatrick, William P. "Black Marketeers and Mani-
       chees: Anthony Burgess' Cold War Novels." West
       Virginia University Bulletin: Philological Papers,
       21 (December 1974), pp. 78-91.

L47   _____. "The Sworn Enemy of Pop: Burgess'
       Mr. Enderby." Bulletin of the West Virginia
       Association of College English Teachers (Marshall
       University), 1, No. 1 (1974), pp. 28-37.

L48   Friedman, Melvin J. "Anthony Burgess and James
       Joyce: A Literary Confrontation." Literary Crite-
       rion, 9, No. 4 (Summer 1971), pp. 71-83.

L49   Fulkerson, Richard P. "Teaching A Clockwork
       Orange." CEA Critic, 37, No. 1 (November 1974),
       pp. 8-10.

L50   Fussell, B. H. "Fed Up to Here." Letter. New
      York Times Book Review, 10 November 1968,
      p. 52. Reply to Burgess's "Fed Up to Here"
      [G104].

L51   Gaughan, Norbert F. "Anthony Burgess." Letter.
      Times Literary Supplement, 7 September 1973,
      p. 1028.

L52   Gilbert, Basil. "Kubrick's Marmalade: The Art of
      Violence." Meanjin, 33 (1974), pp. 157-62.

L53   Gleneak, William. "Diminishing Returns." Letter.
      New York Times Magazine, 29 July 1973, pp. 2,
      4. Reply to Burgess's "For Permissiveness with
      Misgivings" [G111].

L54   Halebsky, Nat. "Pubbing and Dubbing in the Baaaaalmy
      'Other England.'" Letter. New York Times, 25
      February 1973, Travel and Leisure Section, p. 4.
      Response to Burgess's "In the Other England, the
      Land of Cotton, Nobody Says Baaaaath" [G169].

L55   Hamalian, Leo. "Anthony Burgess at Fordham."
      Times Literary Supplement, 10 August 1973, p. 931.
      See also Burgess's 22 June 1973 "Viewpoint" [G440]
      and replies from George W. Shea [L106] and Brian
      Stone [L111].

L56   Handler, M. S. "Lillian Hellman Is Among Nine
      Named to City University Chairs." New York
      Times, 26 September 1972, p. 38. Burgess men-
      tioned as one of the nine. Reference to his serving
      as a Distinguished Professor at CUNY.

L57   Hanff, Helene. "Choking on Names." Letter. New
      York Times Magazine, 29 August 1976, p. 46.
      Response to Burgess's "Dirty Words" [G85].

L58   Harris, Wilson. "Ugh." Letter. Times Literary

About Burgess: Articles, Essays / 139

Supplement, 9 January 1964, p. 27. Response to
Burgess's "In Defense of William Burroughs" [G167].

L59   Hess, John L. "Prof. Burgess, Your Humble Nar-
        rator of Joyce." New York Times 15 September
        1972, p. 39.

L60   Hicks, Granville. "Fertile World of Anthony Burgess."
        Saturday Review, 15 July 1967, pp. 27-29, 36.
        Same as review of [A04], [A09], and [A15].

L61   Isaacs, Neil D. "Unstuck in Time: Clockwork Orange
        and Slaughterhouse-Five." Literature-Film Quar-
        terly, 1, No. 2 (April 1973), pp. 122-31.

L62   Isnard, Marcel. "Anthony Burgess." Etudes Anglaises,
        19 (January-March 1966), pp. 45-54.

L63   Janssen, Otto. "Pubbing and Dubbing in the Baaaaalmy
        'Other England.'" Letter. New York Times, 25
        February 1973, Travel and Leisure Section, p. 4.
        Response to Burgess's "In the Other England, the
        Land of Cotton, Nobody Says Baaaaath" [G169].

L64   Johnson, Stephen L. "Pubbing and Dubbing in the
        Baaaaalmy 'Other England.'" Letter. New York
        Times, 25 February 1973, Travel and Leisure
        Section, p. 4. Response to Burgess's "In the
        Other England, the Land of Cotton, Nobody Says
        Baaaaath" [G169].

L65   Kahn, David A. "G. B. S., O.M." Letter. New
        York Times Magazine, 21 December 1969, p. 26.
        Response to Burgess's "Seen Any Good Galsworthy
        Lately?" [G361].

L66   Kahn, Herman. "Books They Liked Best." Book
        World, 8 December 1967, p. 16. Lists A Clock-
        work Orange [A04] and The Wanting Seed [A30]
        among his favorites of 1967.

L67   K[arp], W[alter]. "The Clockwork Society." Horizon,
       15 (Winter 1973), pp. 2-3. The different views
       and dueling weapons of B. F. Skinner and Anthony
       Burgess. Introductory comments for Burgess's
       "A Fable for Social Scientists" [G103].

L68   Kateb, George. "Politics and Modernity: The Strate-
       gies of Desperation." New Literary History, 3
       (Autumn 1971), pp. 93-111.

L69   Kauffman, Stanley. "Literature of the Early Sixties."
       Wilson Library Bulletin, 39, No. 9 (May 1965),
       pp. 748-77.

L70   Kennard, Jean. "MF: A Separable Meaning." River-
       side Quarterly, 6 (1975), pp. 200-06.

L71   Kronemeyer, Warren. "Think!" Letter. New York
       Times, 18 May 1975, Sect. 2, p. 19. Reply to
       Burgess's "On the Hopelessness of Turning Good
       Books into Films" [G298].

L72   Leavis, Ralph. "Beethoven." Letter. Times Liter-
       ary Supplement, 17 June 1977, p. 733. Response
       to Burgess's comments on Beethoven, in his "The
       Prince of Percussion" [G329].

L73   LeClair, Thomas. "Essential Opposition: The Novels
       of Anthony Burgess." Critique: Studies in Modern
       Fiction, 12, No. 3 (1971), pp. 77-94.

L74   Letter. Times (London), 23 April 1977, p. 15.
       Response to Burgess's "Orwell's 1984" [G301].

L75   Letter. Times Literary Supplement, 7 October 1977,
       p. 1149. Response to Burgess's "Murray and His
       Monument" [G262].

L76   Letter. Times Literary Supplement, 14 October 1977,

p. 1200. Response to Burgess's "Murray and His
Monument" [G262].

L77 McCormick, Anne H. "Meeting New York Realistically." Letter. New York Times Magazine, 19
November 1972, p. 34. Response to Burgess's
"Anthony Burgess Meets New York" [G10]. Burgess's response to this letter appears on the same
page [G204].

L78 McCracken, Samuel. "Novels into Film; Novelist into
Critic: A Clockwork Orange ... Again." Antioch
Review, 32 (June 1974), pp. 427-36.

L79 Manning, Mrs. Robert N. "Pubbing and Dubbing in
the Baaaaalmy 'Other England.'" Letter. New
York Times, 25 February 1973, Travel and Leisure
Section, p. 4. Response to Burgess's "In the
Other England, the Land of Cotton, Nobody Says
Baaaaath" [G169].

L80 Menuhin, Yehudi. "Unfinished Journey." Letter.
Times Literary Supplement, 22 April 1977, p. 488.
Response to Burgess's review of Menuhin's Un-
finished Journey [G446].

L81 Milic, Louis T. "Keep Trying, Mac." Letter. New
York Times Magazine, 30 September 1973, p. 8.
Reply to Burgess's "Ameringlish Isn't Britglish"
[G04].

L82 Mitchell, Julian. "Anthony Burgess." London Magazine, 3 (November 1973), pp. 48-54.

L83 Montemore, Miles. "The Innocents." Letter. New
York Times, 18 May 1975, Sect. 2, p. 19. Reply
to Burgess's "On the Hopelessness of Turning
Good Books into Films" [G298].

L84 Morgan, Edwin. "Belli in Translation." Letter.

Times Literary Supplement, 7 November 1975, p. 1332. Response to Burgess's "Writing in Rome." [G472].

L85 Murdoch, B. "The Overpopulated Wasteland: Myth in Anthony Burgess' The Wanting Seed." Revue des Langues Vivantes, 39 (1973), pp. 203-17.

L86 Nichols, Lewis. "Mr. Burgess." New York Times Book Review, 10 April 1966, p. 8.

L87 "Notes on People." New York Times, 10 March 1972, p. 48. A paragraph stating that Burgess will serve as a writer and consultant to the Tyrone Guthrie Theatre.

L88 Oates, Joyce Carol. "Anthony Burgess's Viewpoint." Letter. Times Literary Supplement, 13 April 1973, p. 420. Response to Burgess's 23 March 1973 "Viewpoint" [G437].

L89 Pace, Eric. "Fears of Local Censorship Haunt the Book Trade." New York Times, 8 January 1974, p. 26. An article on censorship that mentions A Clockwork Orange [A04].

L90 Page, Malcolm. "Anthony Burgess: The Artist as Performer." West Coast Review, 4, No. 3 (January 1970), pp. 21-24.

L91 Page, W. F. "Earwicker." Letter. Times Literary Supplement, 27 July 1973, p. 869. Refers to 15 June review of Joysprick [D15] and the name Earwicker.

L92 Plank, Robert. "The Place of Evil in Science Fiction." Extrapolation: A Journal of Science Fiction and Fantasy, 14, No. 2 (May 1973), pp. 100-11.

L93 Plant, Wilson. "Ugh." Letter. Times Literary Supplement, 9 January 1964, p. 27. Response to Burgess's "In Defense of William Burroughs" [G167].

L94 Porter, Horace A. "To Do One's Own Thinking." Letter. New York Times Magazine, 24 December 1972, p. 32. Letter addressed to Burgess in response to Burgess's "My Dear Students" [G265].

L95 Pottle, Frederick A. "Burns's Scots." Letter. Times Literary Supplement, 14 October 1977, p. 1200. Refers to Burgess's "Murray and His Monument" [G262].

L96 Pritchard, William H. "The Novels of Anthony Burgess." Massachusetts Review, (Summer 1966), pp. 525-39.

L97 Raban, Jonathan. "What Shall We Do About Anthony Burgess?" Encounter, 43 (November 1974), pp. 83-88. Same as reviews [A07] and [A22].

L98 Rebanks, Leslie. "Exile's Doggerel." Letter. New York Times, 25 March 1973, Travel and Leisure Section, p. 24. Reply to Burgess's "In the Other England, the Land of Cotton, Nobody Says Baaaaath" [G169].

L99 Ricks, Christopher. "The Epicene." New Statesman, 5 April 1963, p. 496. A review article. See also Honey for the Bears [A15] and The Novel To-Day [D21].

L100 "Rubenstein Cited with Burgess." New York Times, 15 May 1973, p. 29. Burgess to be awarded the National Arts Club's Sixth Annual Award in Literature.

L101 Samuels, Charles Thomas. "The Context of A Clockwork Orange" [Film]. American Scholar, 41 (Summer 1972), pp. 439-43.

L102 Saunders, Trevor J. "Plato's Clockwork Orange." Durham University Journal, 68 (June 1976), pp. 113-17.

L103 Sauveur, Mrs. F. St. "An Only Child Remembers." Letter. New York Times, 20 July 1977, Sect. C, p. 6. Response to Burgess's "Growing Up an Only Child" [G143].

L104 Schrank, Joseph. "Henry Miller." Letter. New York Times Book Review, 27 February 1972, p. 22. Response to Burgess's 2 January 1972 review of Henry Miller's My Life and Times [G282].

L105 Severin-Lounsberry, Barbara. "Holden and Alex: A Clockwork from the Rye?" Four Quarters, 22 No. 4 (Summer 1973), pp. 27-38.

L106 Shea, George W. "Anthony Burgess at Fordham." Letter. Times Literary Supplement, 20 July 1973, p. 834. See also Burgess's 22 June 1973 "Viewpoint" [G439] and responses by Leo Hamalian [L54] and Brian Stone [L110].

L107 Stinson, John J. "Anthony Burgess: Novelist on the Margin." Journal of Popular Culture, 7, No. 1 (Summer 1973), pp. 136-51.

L108 _____. "The Manichee World of Anthony Burgess." Renascene, 26, No. 1 (Autumn 1973), pp. 37-47.

L109 _____. "Nothing Like the Sun: The Faces in Bella Cohen's Mirror." Journal of Modern Literature, 5, No. 1 (1976), pp. 31-47.

L110 _____. "Waugh and Anthony Burgess: Some Notes

Toward an Assessment of Influence and Affinities."
Evelyn Waugh Newsletter, 10, No. 3 (1976), pp. 11-
12.

L111 Stone, Brian. "American Students." Letter. _Times_
Literary Supplement, 6 July 1973, p. 779. Reply
to Burgess's 22 June 1973 "Viewpoint" [G440].

L112 Sullivan, Walter. "Death Without Tears: Anthony
Burgess and the Dissolution of the West." _Hollins_
Critic, 6, No. 2 (April 1969), pp. 1-11.

L113 _Sunday Times,_ 11 March 1973, p. 48.

L114 Swann, Nancy. "Goring the Ox." Letter. _New York_
Times Magazine, 29 August 1976, p. 46. Response
to Burgess's "Dirty Words" [G85].

L115 Taub, Sheila. "Just How Innocent?" Letter. _New_
York Times Magazine, 29 August 1976, p. 46.
Response to Burgess's "Dirty Words" [G85].

L116 Thundy, Zacharias P. "Cwēn's English." Letter.
Times Literary Supplement, 25 February 1977,
p. 215. Response to Burgess's "In the Year of
Jubilee" [G170].

L117 "2.5 Million Pound TV Series on Life of Shakespeare."
Times (London), 6 February 1973, p. 1. A series
based on Burgess's _Shakespeare_ [D26] to be shown
in twelve one-hour episodes.

L118 Umans, Robert S. "The Novel." Letter. _New York_
Times Book Review, 6 September 1964, p. 18.
Response to Burgess's "A Novelist's Sources Are
Myth, Language and the Here-and-Now" [G291].

L119 "University of Rochester Pays Tribute to Benefactor."

New York Times, 11 November 1972, p. 67. Brief
reference to Burgess, who gave a lecture as part
of the tribute to Joseph C. Wilson, deceased, who
was honorary chairman of the board of trustees of
the University of Rochester.

L120   Updike, John. Letter. Commonweal, 22 April 1966,
pp. 160-61. Answers Burgess's criticism [G198]
of the language used in certain paragraphs of Of the
Farm. "Mr. Burgess, like less sympathetic critics, assumes that I regard language as a kind of
third force, lovable in itself. Actually, nothing
about language interests me except its possibilities
for precision. "

L121   Waldo, D. E. "Fed Up to Here. " Letter. New York
Times Book Review, 10 November 1968, p. 52.
Reference to Burgess's "Fed Up to Here" [G104].

L122   Walker, Keith. "Johnson's Dictionary. " Letter.
Times Literary Supplement, 8 October 1977, p. 1149.
Response to Burgess's "Murray and His Monument"
[G262].

L123   Weiler, A. H. "Whistle a Tune from Thomas Mann. "
New York Times, 3 June 1973, Sect. 2, p. 11.
Anthony Burgess and Stephen Schwartz to collaborate
on a musical film version of The Transposed Head,
by Thomas Mann.

L124   Weinkauf, Mary. "The God Figure in Dystopian Fiction. " Riverside Quarterly, 4, No. 4 (March
1971), pp. 266-71.

L125   Wood, Michael. "A Dream of Clockwork Oranges. "
New Society, 6 June 1968, pp. 842-43.

L126   "Zeffirelli to Direct a TV Life of Christ. " Times
(London), 31 July 1974, p. 18. See also "The
Gospel According to Anthony Burgess" [G133].

M. BIBLIOGRAPHIES

M01 Boytinck, Paul. Anthony Burgess: An Enumerative
     Bibliography with Selected Annotations. [?]: Nor-
     wood Editions, 1974. [?]: Norwood Editions,
     1977. 2nd edition, with a foreword by Anthony
     Burgess.

M02 David, Beverly R. "Anthony Burgess: A Checklist
     (1956-1971)." Twentieth Century Literature, 19
     (July 1973), pp. 181-88.

M03 Holte, Carlton. "Additions to 'Anthony Burgess: A
     Checklist (1956-1971.'" Twentieth Century Liter-
     ature, 20 (January 1974), pp. 44-52.

LATE ADDITIONS
(not indexed)

ABBA ABBA. Little, Brown, 1977. 1st American edition.

A CHRISTMAS RECIPE. Illus. by Fulvio Testa. Verona: Plain Wrapper Press, 1977. [Limited edition]

"Creeping Towards Salvation. " Times Literary Supplement, 23 November 1979, p. 11.

Review of Shikasta, by Doris Lessing

MAN OF NAZARETH. New York: McGraw-Hill, 1979.

"The People's English. " Times Literary Supplement, 27 October 1978, p. 1255.

Review of The Linguistic Atlas of England, edited by Harold Orton, Stewart Sanderson and John Widdowson.

"The Santa Claus Story. " Times Literary Supplement, 21 December 1979, p. 149.

Review of Charles W. Jones's St. Nicholas of Myra, Bari, and Manhattan.

"Something Lyrical, Something Terrible. " Times Literary Supplement, 26 May 1978, p. 576.

Review of Nonsense and Wonder: The Poems and Cartoons of Edward Lear, by Thomas Byrom.

WILL AND TESTAMENT: A FRAGMENT OF BIOGRAPHY.
[A story about William Shakespeare.] Screenprints by Joe
Tilson. Verona: Plain Wrapper Press, 1977. [Limited
edition]

NAME INDEX

Adams, J. Donald D17
Adams, P.-L. A02, D03
Adams, Phoebe A07, A21, A25,
D26, E01
Adams, R. M. A15
Adler, Dick L01
Aggeler, Geoffrey A11, L02-
L08
Alderman, William L09
Allen, Bruce A07
Alpert, Hollis A05
Amis, Kingsley A15
Amis, Martin A01, A23
Anderson, Ken L10
Arnold, Voiza Olson K01
Arthens, Edith A28
Austin, Charles M. A05

Bagnell, Nicholas D01
Baldwin, Barry A13
Barnes, Clive E01, E02
Bashford, Henry Howarth D09
Baumbach, Elinor A09, A29
Baxter, Ralph C. A10
Bayley, John A22
Beatty, Jack D03
Belmont, Georges A04, A14,
A30
Benstock, Bernard F04
Bentley, Nicholas L14
Bergonzi, Bernard A04, A10,
A18, D19, J01, J02
Berlins, Marcel L15
Betts, Ernest L16
Biggby, C. W. E. J08
Blake, Caesar D15
Blish, James F04
Bliven, Naomi A26, A28
Blythe, Ronald A22
Bolger, Eugenie A13
Bolton, Whitney French D29
Bonicelli, Vittoria L13

Bordwell, H. A04
Bossi, Floriana A04, A10
Bowen, John A09, A15
Bowman, Sylvia E. J06
Boytinck, Paul W. M01
Brickner, R. P. A25
Broadwater, Bowden A10
Brooke, Jocelyn A15, A16,
A29
Brooke-Rose, Christine L17
Brophy, Brigid A30
Brophy, Elizabeth L18
Brown, Francis D23, D25
Brown, Ivor D26
Brown, Les L19
Brown, Rexford Glenn K02
Browne, Joseph D27
Broyard, Anatole A07
Brumm, Walter A04, A07
Buitenhuis, Peter A24, A30
Burgess, Anthony (review by)
A05, A16 (See also Kell,
Joseph)
Burgess, Llewela E04
Burroughs, William L14, L93
Butler, Francelia D26
Byatt, A. S. A07
Byrne, K. L22

Canaday, John F01
Canto, Patricio A28
Canton, Robert F. A30
Carson, Julie L23
Cartey, Wilfred L24
Carvalho, Alredo Leme Coelho
de L25
Cary, Joyce K05
Cerquira, E. G. A21
Charbrier, Hortense A04,
A14, A30
Cheshire, David A21
Chew, Shirley L26

Chipchase, Paul   A22
Ciglic, M.   A05
Citrin, Marion   L27
Cleworth, Joan   L28
Close, R. A.   D17
Coleman, J.   A10, A29
Coleman, John   A26
Collier, John   D11
Comuzio, E.   A05
Connelly, Wayne C.   L29
Cook, Bruce   A28
Cook, Margaret C.   D17
Cooper, Arthur   A25
Corcoran, Neil   L30
Crinklaw, Don   A28
Cromie, A.   A28
Cross, Jack   D03
Cruttwell, Patrick   A18
Crystal, David   D29
Cullinan, John (Thomas)   K03,
   L31-L33
Curley, Dorothy   A10
Cutler, Edward J.   D27

Dahlie, Hallvard   L34
Daiches, David   C03
Damant, David   L35
d'Amico, Suso Cecchi   A17
Daniel, John   A28
Daniels, D.   A05
Davenport, Guy   A10
David, Beverly R.   M02
Davis, Earle   L36
Davis, L. J.   A13
Davis, Robert Gorham   A04, A28
DeMott, Benjamin   A10, A21,
   D26
Dempsey, David   A30
Denby, David   A05
Derrick, Christopher   L37
Desani, Govindas Vishnaodas
   D08
Deutsch, Michel   A28
DeVitis, A. A.   J06
Dick, Bernard F.   L38
Dick, Kay   A13
Dick, Susan   D27
Dimeo, Steven   L39
Dix, Carol M.   J07
Dolbier, M.   A28, D17
Dollen, Charles   A28
Donadio, Stephen   A21
Donleavy, J. P.   K08

Donley, Michael   L40
Donoghue, Denis   A09, D07,
   D24
Doyle, Arthur Conan   D14
Doyle, Paul A.   D27
Driver, C. J.   A01
Duchene, A.   A28
Duffey, Martha   A21
Durrell, Lawrence   K05

Eagleton, Terry   D26
Eastman, Arthur M.   D15
Eckley, Grace   D16
Edel, Leon   F04
Edelstein, J. M.   L41
Edwards, T.   A07
Elledge, Jim   A23
Elsaesser, Thomas   J08
Engelborghs, Maurits   J09
English, Hubert M., Jr.   D15
Enright, D. J.   A24, J10
Evans, Fallon   A28
Evans, Robert O.   L42, L43

Feeney, William J.   D27
Fernando, Lloyd   L44
Fink, John   A26
Fiore, Peter Amadeus   L45
Fisher, Antonia   D18
Fitzpatrick, William P.   L46,
   L47
Fleischer, L.   A09, A18
Fletcher, C.   C03
Foote, Audrey   A25
Foote, Timothy   A07
Ford, B.   F01
Fox, Jay   D16
Fraser, G. S.   A23
Fremont-Smith, E.   D24
Frezzato, A.   A05
Friedman, Melvin J.   J11,
   J13, L48
Fukada, Rikutaro   D02
Fulkerson, Richard P.   L49
Furbank, P. N.   D07
Fussell, B. H.   L50

Gabriel, Brother D.   A18
Galsworthy, John   L65
Gambetti, G.   A05
Gardner, John   A28, A29
Garrett, George   A24
Gaster, Brian   J15

Gaughan, Norbert F. L51
Gavin, William F. A15
Gilbert, Basil L52
Glendenning, Victoria A22
Gleneak, William L53
Golding, William K08
Goldman, Arnold D16
Gosling, Ray D17
Gotfart, Dorothea A15
Granetz, Marc A23
Graver, Lawrence A28
Green, Martin A11
Greene, Graham D23
Gress, Elsa A04
Grigson, Geoffrey A09, D20,
D27, J12
Gross, J. F04
Gross, John A08, A15
Grumenik, Arthur A05

Hackett, A. A29, D24
Halebsky, Nat L54
Halio, Jay L. A22, A24
Hamalian, Leo L55
Hamilton, A. A15, A30
Handler, M. S. L56
Hanff, Helene L57
Harris, L. A28
Harris, Wilson L58
Harrison, Joseph G. D17
Hart, Clive D07
Harte, Barbara J34
Harvey, David D. A15
Hatch, Robert A05, A24, D28
Hess, John L. L59
Hicks, Granville A04, A09,
A10, A15, D19, L60
Hiltmen, E. A05
Hisaya, Kuroyanagi A30
Hodgart, Matthew D07, D24,
F04
Hoffman, A. C. J13
Hoffman, Charles G. J13
Hoffman, Frederick J. J13
Hoggart, R. D19
Hollis, Christopher D07
Holmes, Richard A11
Holte, Carlton Thomas K04,
M03
Honour, H. F01
Horrocks, Norman A21
Howes, Alan B. D15
Hoyt, Charles Alva A15, A29

Hughes, Douglas A. D28
Hughes, Robert A05
Huish, Lois F04
Hyman, Stanley J14

Irwin, Michael A23
Irwin, W. R. J17
Isnard, Marcel L62
Issacs, Neil D. L61
Ivask, Ivar J18
Ivsky, Oleg A15

Jackson, Burgess A05
Jamal, Zahir A23
James, Clive A23
Janssen, Otto L63
Jebb, Julian A08
Jennings, Elizabeth A08, A24
Johnson, J. J. A21
Johnson, Joseph J. J19
Johnson, Stephen L. L64
Josselson, Diana A04
Joyce, James D16

Kael, Pauline A05
Kahn, David A. L65
Kahn, Herman L66
Kain, R. M. D23
Karl, Frederick R. J20
Karp, Walter L67
Kateb, George L68
Kauffmann, Stanley A05, A18,
A24, L69
Kazue, Saitô A30
Keeney, Willard A09
Kell, Joseph (pseudonym of
Anthony Burgess) A16, A25
Kellogg, Jean A05
Kennard, J. E. J21
Kennard, Jean L70
Kennedy, A. R. A26
Keown, Eric A08, A30
Kermode, Frank A16, A21
Kerr, Walter E02
Khanuitin, I. A05
Kitching, J. A28
Knickerbocker, Conrad A29
Koltz, Newton A07
Korn, E. A02
Kostelanetz, Richard J14
Kronemeyer, Warren L71

Lacy, Allen A23

Lamott, Kenneth A24
Lancaster, Burt L21
Langham, Michael E05
Lask, Thomas D26
Laski, Marghanita A26
Leal, Aníbal A04
Leavis, Ralph L72
LeClair, Thomas L73
Le Guin, Ursula K07
Lehmann-Haupt, Christopher A21
Lejeune, Anthony A28
Lenaghan, Robert T. D15
Lennon, Peter A22
Levey, M. F01
Levin, Martin A04, A08
Levitas, G. A28
Lewald, H. E. D24
Lewis, Naomi D26
Lhamon, W. T. A07
Lindroth, J. B. A09
Lindroth, James R. A13, A21, A28
Lodge, David A02, A15, D19, D20, J22
Loprete, N. J., Jr. D18
Lord, J. A28
Luckett, Richard D16
Lucy, Sean D26
Lundgren, Caj A04, A09, A25, A28

Mablekos, Carole [Marbes] A10, K05
Macauley, Robie D27
McCabe, Bernard A24
McCormack, Thomas D05
McCormick, Anne H. L77
McCracken, Samuel L78
McDowell, Frederick W. P. A10
McInery, Ralph A21
McKenzie, Robb A22
McLellan, Joseph A23
McNamara, Leo F. D15
Maguire, Clinton J. A30
Malin, Irving A09, A10, A15
Maloff, Saul A09, A28
Mamber, S. A05
Mann, Thomas L123
Manning, Robert N. (Mrs.) L79
Mantell, M. I03

Marszalek, R. A05
Mayne, Richard A28
Menuhin, Yehudi L80
Milic, Louis T. L81
Miller, Henry L104
Miller, Walter K07
Miller, Warren A24
Mitchell, James D06
Mitchell, Julian A08, D27, L82
Montemore, Miles L83
Moon, Eric A28
Moore, H. T. A25
Moran, John F. A04
Moran, Kathryn Lou K06
Morgan, Edwin A01, L84
Morris, Robert K. A10, A13, A22, J23
Mortensen, Harry A28
Moynahan, J. A02
Mozart, W. A. D10
Murdoch B. L85
Murdoch, Iris K08
Murray, James L75, L76, L122
Murray, John J. A02, A07, A13, A21, A22
Murray, Patrick D20

Nash, Manning A21
Newlove, Donald D18
Nichols, Lewis L86
Nicol, Charles A07
Noel, Bernard D26
Noon, William T. D24
Nordell, Roderick A22, A23, A26
Nowell, Robert A11, A21
Nye, Robert A07

Oages, Joyce Carol L88
O'Dea, Richard J. D24
O'Hara, J. D. A07, A22
Oilmarks, Ake A24
O'Malley, Michael A10
Orwell, George D13, L74
Ostermann, R. A07, A09, A10, A18, A28, A29
Ott, William D03

Pace, Eric L89
Page, Malcolm L90
Page, Norman J25

Page, W. F.   L91
Paulin, T.   A01
Peake, Mervyn   D13
Pechter, William S.   A05
Pelegri, Jean   E06
Perreault, John   F01
Petersen, C.   A26
Pettingell, Phoebe   A10
Pippett, Aileen   A24
Plank, Robert   L92
Plant, Wilson   L93
Platypus, Bill   A15, A16, A21,
   A22, A30
Plummer, Christopher   E02
Poirer, Richard   D24
Porter, Horace A.   L94
Porter, Raymond   D24
Potter, Dennis   D26
Pottle, Frederick A.   L95
Prescott, Peter S.   A07, A23
Price, Martin   A08
Price, R. G.   A10
Price, R. G. G.   A26, A31
Prince, Peter   A07
Pritchard, W. H.   A02, A07,
   A10, A28, D19, L96

Quigley, Isabel   A08

Raban, Jonathan   A07, A21,
   A22, L97
Rabinovitz, Rubin   J26
Rabinowitz, Dorothy   A07
Ratcliffe, Michael   A20, A22
Raven, Simon   A31
Raymond, J.   A24
Raymond, John   A26
Rea, Robert   F01
Ready, William   A09, A28
Rebanks, Leslie   L98
Rees, D.   A10
Rees, Davis   A11
Revzin, Philip   A23
Reynolds, S.   A10
Richardson, M.   A28
Richardson, Maurice   A09
Rickleft, R.   D17
Ricks, Christopher   A01, A02,
   A05, A15, A21, D29, L99
Riley, Carolyn   J34
Rodgers, W. R.   D07
Rogers, Pat   A02
Rogers, W. G.   A08

Ronald, Paul   A17
Rosier, James   D15
Rosofsky, H. L.   A09
Rostand, Edmond   E01, E02
Ryan, Stephen P.   A24

Saint-Pierre, Michel de
   E04
Sale, Roger   A22, A24, D19
Samuels, Charles Thomas
   A05, L101
Sanborn, Sara   A22
Sarivonova, M.   A05
Saunders, Trevor J.   L102
Sauveur, F. St. (Mrs.)   L103
Sayre, Ed   A25
Schickel, Richard   A04
Schneider, Rupert   A01
Schoenbaum, Samuel   J27
Scholes, Robert   J29
Schott, Webster   A28
Schrank, Joseph   L104
Schwartz, Stephen   L123
Scott, P.   A01
Scott-Kilvert, Ian   J07
Sears, W. P.   D24
Selby, Hubert, Jr.   D12
Servin, Jean   E03
Severin-Lounsberry, Barbara
   L105
Seymour-Smith, Martin   D07,
   F04, J28
Shakespeare, William   L117
Shea, George W.   L55, L106
Sheppard, R. Z.   A22, A25
Shickel, Richard   A05
Shigeo, Hisashi   D02
Shin'ichiro, Inui   A04
Shone, Richard   D03
Shrapnel, N.   A10
Shrapnel, Norman   A10, A26
Shuttleworth, M.   A29
Siciliano, Sam Joseph   K07
Silverman, Stanley   E05
Simms, Theodore F.   D19
Simonelli, G.   A05
Sissung, Maud   D26
Skinner, B. F.   L67
Smith, Godfrey   A07
Smith, Peter Duval   A03
Soete, M.   A02, C03
Sokolov, R. A.   F01
Solomon, Albert J.   C03

Solotaroff, Theodore A10, J30
Sophocles E05
Staley, Thomas F. D23
Stinson, John Jerome K08,
    L107-L110
Stone, Brian L55, L111
Stone, Donald David J31
Strick, Philip A05
Sullivan, A. M. D23
Sullivan, Walter L112
Swann, Nancy L114
Swanson, Stanley A29
Swenson, E. P. I02

Talbot, Daniel A26
Talbot, David A04
Tannenbaum, Earl A10
Taub, Sheila L115
Taubman, Robert A04, A30
Tennant, Emma A02
Theroux, Paul A02
Thundy, Zacharias P. L116
Tilton, John W. J32
Tisdall, J. A28
Tjen, Michael A30
Toynbee, P. D07
Trewin, Ian A22
Triesch, Gisela D07
Triesch, Manfred D07
Tucker, Martin A28
Tufte, Virginia J33

Umans, Robert S. L118
Updike, John L120
Üstel, Aziz A04
Uusitalo, Inkere A09

Vansittart, Peter A24, A29,
    F01
Vickery, John B. J13
Vinson, James J01
Vonalt, Larry P. D19

Wade, Rosalind A02
Wagner, Kenyon Lewis K09
Wain, John A10
Waldo, D. E. L121
Walker, Keith L122
Wall, Stephen A13
Walters, Raymond, Jr. A04,
    A15, A21, A26, A30, D17
Ward, A. C. J35
Waugh, Auberon A10, A21

Waugh, Evelyn D13, J14
Weiler, A. H. L123
Weinkauf, Mary L124
West, Paul A09, A21
Wheeler, Thomas C. A18,
    A29
Wilkie, Brian A30
Willett, John A28
Williams, David A26
Wilpert, Gero von J18
Wilson, Edmund A25
Wilson, Joseph C. L119
Wilson, Lynn E06
Wiskott, Inge A09
Wood, Frederick T. A29
Wood, Michael C03, L125
Woodcock, George A18
Woods, M. A02

Yuichi, Makawa D19

Zeffirelli, Franco A17, L126
Zelazny, Roger K07
Zimmerman, Paul D. A05
Zivković, Zoran A04

TITLE INDEX

"Abracadabra Man, The" A01
"Additions to 'Anthony Burgess: A Checklist (1956-1971)'" M03
Afterwords: Novelists on Their Novels D05
Agent qui vous veut du bien, Un A28
"Algonquin Legend" A21
"Algonquin Oedipus, The" A21
"All Life Is One" A07
"American Students" L111
"Angry Old Burgess" A02
"Anthony Burgess" H05, J01, J14, L11, L51, L62, L82
"Anthony Burgess: The Artist as Performer" L90
"Anthony Burgess: The Author of A Clockwork Orange Now Switches His Attention to Napoleon's Stomach" H08
"Anthony Burgess: A Checklist (1956-1971)" M02
"Anthony Burgess: Double Vision" J21
Anthony Burgess: An Enumerative Bibliography with Selected Annotations M01
"Anthony Burgess: Novelist on the Margin" L107
"Anthony Burgess: Pushing On" H03
Anthony Burgess. Twayne's English Authors Series J06
Anthony Burgess. Writers and Their Work J07
"Anthony Burgess, The Malayan Trilogy" J23
"Anthony Burgess, MF" J19
"Anthony Burgess' A Clockwork Orange" L31
"Anthony Burgess' 'The Muse: A Sort of SF Story'" L33
"Anthony Burgess's Viewpoint" L31, L88
"Anthony Burgess's Mythopoeic Imagination ..." K09
"Anthony Burgess' Novels: A Critical Introduction" K03
"Anthony Burgess and James Joyce: A Literary Confrontation" L48
"Anthony Burgess Answers Back" H15
"Anthony Burgess at Fordham" L55, L106
"Anthony Longmug?" A23
Apelsin med Urverk, En A04
Appläd med en Hand A25
Approaches to Popular Culture J08
Arancia a Orologeria, Un A04
"Arancia meccanica" A05
"Art of Fiction XLVIII: Anthony Burgess, The" H04
"Art That Pays" H11
"Artist as Hero in the Novels of Joyce Cary, Lawrence Durrell, and Anthony Burgess" K05

157

"As distopias de Anthony Burgess" L25
"Auberon Waugh on New Novels" A21
Augustus Cara, Esq. by Himself D09
"Author Tries Hand at Book Selling" L12
"ATV in 6 Million Pound European Co-Production Venture" L13

"Bands of the Human Spectrum" A08
"Battle Between the Sexes Was the Answer, A" A30
"Beethoven" L72
"Belli in Translation" L84
"Between God and Notgod: Anthony Burgess' Tremor of Intent" L02
"Beyond '1984' But Not Up to It" A23
"Beyond the Pleasure Principle" D27
"Bid and Made" A10
"Black Market in Red Square" A15
"Black Marketeers and Manichees ..." L46
"Bond in Greenland" A28
"Books They Liked Best" L66
"Boor Joyce, The" A10
"Brian Moore: An Interview" L34
"Burgess and Bellow" A24
"Burgess and Gibson" J27
"Burgess and--Kell" L20
"Burgess Memorandum, The" A28
"Burgess on Kubrick on 'Clockwork'" A05
"Burgess to Write Script for 'Moses'" L21
"Burgess vs. Scholes" A10, D19
"Burgess' The Wanting Seed" L32
"Burgess's Many Voices" A02
"Burgess's New Novel" A28
"Burgess's '1985': 7 Years to Cacatopia" A23
"Burgess's Wake" F04
"Burns's Scots" L95
"Busy Hand of Burgess, The" A10
"Busy Hand of Burgess, The" J30
"But the Patient Is Fine" A09

"Candid Interview with the Author of A Clockwork Orange" H17
Canticle for Leibowitz, A K07
"Charlotte, Not Emily" L28
"Chimps, Manikins, People Too" D11
"Choking on Names" L57
"Cineast as Moralizer, The" A05
"Clockwork Kumquat" A25
"Clockwork Orange, A" A04, A05
Clockwork Orange, A (Film) H06
"Clockwork Orange, A: Awareness Is All" J32
"Clockwork Orange, A: English and Nadsat" L18
"Clockwork Orange, A: Novel into Film" A05
"Clockwork Society, The" L67
"Comedy of Discontent, The" A26
"Comic Art of Anthony Burgess, The" L03
"Common Heritage, A" D17

"Conflict and Confluence: The Art of Anthony Burgess" K02
"Consolations of Ambiguity: An Essay on the Novels of Anthony Burgess" J24
Contemporary Authors J03
Contemporary Novelists J01
"Contemporary Novel Through the Eyes of a Pro, The" D19
"Context of A Clockwork Orange, The" A05, L101
Cosmic Satire in the Contemporary Novel J32
"Crack-up" D03
Creatures of Light and Darkness K07
Current Biography J04
Current Biography Yearbook J05
"Current Literature 1965: I. Poetry, Prose, and Drama" A29
"Cwen's English" L116
"Cycle of Cathay, A" A18
Cyrano de Bergerac E02, H01, H04, L12
Cyrano de Bergerac [Stage production] E02
"Cyrano Out of Breath" E02

"Dawn, The Toten, The Drums, The" L24
"Death Without Tears ..." L112
Deo Gratias E03
"Diction Addiction" A09
"Diminishing Returns" L53
"Djunaesque" A04
Doktor ist Übergeschnappt, Der A09
Doktoro är sjuk A09
Dolce bestia, La A10
Don Giovanni and Idomeneo D10
"Dream of Clockwork Oranges, A" L125
"Due tipi de violenza" A05
"Dying to Be Told" A01

"Earwicker" L91
"Eclectic Author of His Own Five Foot Shelf" H10
"Ennead, The" A29
"Enter Will, Dressed in Prose" A24
"Epicene, The" A15, D21, L99
Essays by Linguists and Men of Letters 1858-1964 D29
"Essential Opposition: The Novels of Anthony Burgess" L73
"Everything's Here but the Kievstone Cops" A15
"Exile's Doggerel" L98

"Faces in the Mirror" A02
"Fears of Local Censorship Haunt the Book Trade" L89
"Fed Up to Here" L50, L121
"Fertile World of Anthony Burgess" A04, A09, A15, L60
"Fi, Fi, Fo, Fum" A30
"Fiction and Fabulation" D20
"Fictional Universe of Four Science Fiction Novels, The" K07
"Fifteen Years On ..." A20
"Filling in the Blank Verses of a Man on the Make" A24
"Finnagain" D07

"Flatulent Poet, The" A10
Folle semence, La A30
"Fooling Around, and Serious Business" A22
"For Him the Bell Tolls" D03
"Four Fantasies" A09
"From the Bookshelf" D17
"Funny Book" A04

"G. B. S. , O. M. " L65
Game of the Impossible: A Rhetoric of Fantasy J17
Gendai Shosetsu D19
"Glob and His Guts, A" A10
"God Figure in Dystopian Fiction, The" L124
God I Want, The D06
"Goddess Speaks with a Greek Accent, The" A13
"God's Plenty in a Flood of Proper and Improper Nouns" A21
"Gog into Vision" A10
"Going Red" A15
"Goring the Ox" L114
Grammar as Style J33

"Haveth Critics Everywhere" D07
"Help!" A05
"Henry Miller" L104
"Heroes of Our Time" A11
"High Hack" D27
"Higher Games" A21
"His Fame Proceeds in Giant Steps" D24
"Holden and Alex: A Clockwork from the Rye?" L105
Hoois für die Bären A15
"Horror Show" A11
"House of Burgesses" A28
"House of Fiction" D20
"Hungry Sheep, The" A30

"I Love England, but I Will No Longer Live There" H13
Igirisu Bungakushi D02
"Imperial Rag" A22
"Imperial Theme" A22
"In the Other England, the Land of Cotton, Nobody Says Baaaaath"
  L63, L79
"Incest and the Artist: Anthony Burgess's MF as Summation" L04
"Incest in the Widest Sense" A21
"Innocents, The" L83
"Insatiable Liking" D20, D27
"Inside Mr. Burgess" L01
International Authors and Writers Who's Who J15
International Who's Who, 1978-79 J16
"Interview in New York with Anthony Burgess, An" H01
"Interview with Anthony Burgess, An" H02
"Interview with Anthony Burgess, An" H18
Intet Är Som Solen: En Berättelse om Shakespeares Käreksliv A24
"Invaded Selves" A28

"Jakes Peer or Jacques Pere" A24
"James Joyce" D07, D16
John Collier Reader D11
"Johnson's Dictionary" L122
"Journey of Diligence" F01
"Joyce the Great" D07
"Joyce Tri-umphant" D24
"Joyce's Burgessbook" D07
"Joyous Cynicism" A28
"Jumble Shelf, The" F02
"Just How Innocent?" L115

"Keep Trying, Mac" L81
"Kenelle kellopeli soi" A05
"Konfrontatsiia--Varsheva 73" A05
"Koshmart na bdesheto" A05
"Kubrick Country" A05
"Kubrick's Brilliant Vision" A05
"Kubrick's Horrorshow" A05
"Kubrick's Marmalade: The Art of Violence" L52

"Language" D17
Last Exit to Brooklyn D12
"Laugh Now--Think Later! The Genius of Anthony Burgess" L36
"Lawyers Reject Author's Attack" L15
"Lillian Hellman Is Among Nine Named to City University Chairs" L56
"Literary English in the South-East Asian Tradition" L44
"Literature of the Early Sixties" L69
"Local Boys Make Good" A26
Longman Companion to Twentieth Century Literature J35
"Love and the Grotesque" A22
"Ludwig Van e gli altri" A05
"Lusty Man Was Will, A" A24

Macho & Fêmea A21
"Making of a Monument, The" D26
"Man Is an Onion: Reviews and Essays" J10
Mann in Dublin Namens Joyce, Ein D07
"Mannichee World of Anthony Burgess, The" L108
Martyrernes Blod A28
"Matter of Concern, A" A09
"Mechanicna oranza" A05
"Meeting New York Realistically" L77
"Middle-Browed Faction" A15
Mikomo No Nai Shushi A30
"Milk-Plus and Ultra Violence" A05
"Millions on a Musical about Shakespeare" L16
"Milton or Kubrick: Eden's Apple or a Clockwork Orange" L45
"Mr. Burgess" L86
"Mr. Enderby and Mr. Burgess" A11, L05
"Mr. Kell and Mr. Burgess: Inside and Outside Mr. Enderby" J13
"Mr. Livedog's Day: The Novels of Anthony Burgess" L26

"Mr. W. S. " A24
"Modern Disease: Anthony Burgess's Shakespeare, A" J10
"Morality with Heart" A26
"More Big 1967 Books" F01
"More Fiction Writing Tips" H07
"More Smog from the Dark Satanic Mills" A28
"Mugging Machine, The" H06
"Murdoch's Eighth" A13
"Music Week" A26
My Life and Times L104
"MF: A Separable Meaning" L70

"Nadsat: The Argot and Its Implications in Anthony Burgess' A
    Clockwork Orange" L42
Naranja mecánica, La A04
"Narrative Structure and the Readers Theatre Staging of Nothing
    Like the Sun by Anthony Burgess" K01
New Movements in the Study and Teaching of English D01
"New Order of Things, A" A28
"No Bardolatry" A24
"No Invitation to Tea" D24
"Noia, La" A08
Norton Reader: An Anthology of Expository Prose, The D15
"Not for Reading" L27
"Not Very Brave, Not So New" A30
"Notes on People" H12
"Nothing Like the English" D19
"Nothing Like the Sun: The Faces in Bella Cohen's Mirror" L109
"Nouveau Roman, Russian Dystopias, and Anthony Burgess, The"
    L43
Nouveaux aristocrates, Le E04
"Novel, The" L118
"Novel Picture, A" D26
"Novel Today and Tomorrow, The" D19
Novelist at the Crossroads and Other Essays on Fiction and Criticism
    J22
Novels in a Changing World J31
"Novels into Film; Novelist into Critic ... " L78
"Novels of Anthony Burgess, The" L96
"NBC Buys Anglo-Italian Series on the Life of Jesus" L19

"O Brave New Worlds" A23
Of the Farm L120
"Of Time and Literature" D19
Oliviers de la justice, Le E06
"On Being a Lancashire Catholic" H20
"On Collecting One's Reviews" J12
"On Leave and On the Job" A26
"On the Move" A02
"Only Child Remembers, An" L103
"Optimism in Burgess's A Clockwork Orange" L29
L'orange mécanique A04
"Ordeals and Orgies" A26

Otamatik portakal A04
"Overpopulated Wasteland: Myth in A. B.'s The Wanting Seed" L85

"Package Tour" A21
Page 2: The Best of "Speaking of Books" from the New York Times
 Book Review" D23, D25
Paklena pomorandža A04
"Palace 'Cyrano' Opens March 25" E02
"Paperbacks" A16
"Peckinpah and Kubrick: Fire and Ice" A05
"Pelagius and Augustine in the Novels of Anthony Burgess" L06
"Perilous Balance, The" A04
Perspectives on Pornography D28
"Picaresque and Gawky" A15
Pipopää Potilas A09
"Place of Evil in Science Fiction, The" L92
"Plato's Clockwork Orange" L102
"Playboy Interview: Anthony Burgess" H16
"Plum Pudding" F02
"Plummer Triumphs in Musical 'Cyrano'" E02
"Poetry and Borborygms" A16
"Poetry and Defense" A10
"Poetry Can Kill a Man" A07
"Poet's Life, A" A10
"Politics and Modernity: The Strategies of Desperation" L68
"Pop Nihilism at the Movies" A05
"Preaching Polyglottism" D17
"Primary Colours" A24
"Prof. Burgess, Your Humble Narrator of Joyce" L59
"Professor's Pajama Games" A09
"Pronominalization in A Clockwork Orange" L23
"Prophetic Acrostic in Anthony Burgess' Nothing Like the Sun" L07
"Prospects" A30
"Provincial Champions and Grandmasters" A24
"Pubbing and Dubbing in the Baaaaalmy 'Other England'" L54, L63,
 L79

Reaction Against Experiment in the English Novel, 1950-1960 J26
Reader's Guide to the Contemporary English Novel, A J20
"Recent British Fiction: Some Established Writers" A10
"Richard Luckett on Joyce, Beckett and the Word" D16
"Ripeness Is All ... " A09
"Riproposta della vita" A05
"Roman Experimental en Angleterre, Le" L17
"Romans van een Woordkunstenaar" J09
"Rubenstein Cited with Burgess" L100
"Rude Forerunner" A29

"Sanctification of the Ordinary, The" D24
"Satiric Ramble" A30
"Say It with Paperbacks" A04, A15, A21, A26, A30
"Schizoids in Leningrad" A15
"Screen Violence: Emotional Structure and Ideological Function in
 A Clockwork Orange" J08

"Seat of Pleasure" A10
"Sense of the Present, A" A24
"Set to Beethoven" A22
"Sex in Print" A15
Shaken Realist, The: Essays in Modern Literature in Honor of
   Frederic J. Hoffman J13
"Shakespeare: The Works and the Worker" D26
"Shakespeare and the Readers" D26
"Shakespeare Panorama" D26
"Sin Was a Chronic Disease" A28
Skal Aede din Naeste, Du A30
Skuggen ar ett Svek A28
"Small Brilliance, A" A01
"Small Dose of Joyce, A" F04
"Some Elegant Essays" D27
"Sonneteer Was Not All Talk, The" A24
"Sparing the Rod" A31
Speech in the English Novel J25
"Spy in the Sky" A28
"Spying, the Cold War and Eschatology" A28
"Stanley Strangelove" A05
"Stirring the Guttywuts" A05
"Stoked-Up 1976, A" A23
"Stranded on Gibralter" A29
Structural Fabulation: An Essay on Fiction of the Future J29
"Sworn Enemy of Pop, The: Burgess' Mr. Enderby" L47
Symphonie Napoléon, Le A22

"Tale of Two Cities" D18
"Taming the Rock: Myth, Model and Metaphor in the Novels of
   Anthony Burgess" K04
"Teaching A Clockwork Orange" L48
Testament de l'orange, Le A07
"There Is No Place for Home" L22
"Thing's the Thing, The" A01
"Think!" L71
"This Our Exile: The Novels of Anthony Burgess" L37
"Ticking of an Orange, The" L39
Titus Groan D13
"To Do One's Own Thinking" L94
"To Russia with Torment" A15
Tokei Jikake No Orenji A04
"Tour of the Pops, A" A28
"Translation" L40
Transposed Head, The L123
"Travel" F01
Trémula Intención A28
"Trombone on Fire, A" A21
"Tucland, Their Tucland" A23
"'Tukland': Grim Alternate to Orwell's Future" A23
"Twilight of Empire in the Malay States" A18
"2. 5 Million Pound TV Series on Life of Shakespeare" L117
200 Contemporary Authors J34

"Ugh" L35, L58, L93
Uhrwerk Orange A04
Uhrwerk-Testament, Das A07
Ultima missão A28
"Ultimate Spy, The" A28
"Unavoidable Whimsy" A13
"Unfinished Journey" L80
"University of Rochester Pays Tribute to Benefactor" L119
"Unstuck in Time: Clockwork Orange and Slaughterhouse-Five" L61
"Uses of the Grotesque and other Modes of Distortion: Philosophy
    and Implications in the Novels of Iris Murdoch, William Golding,
    Anthony Burgess, and J. P. Donleavy" K08
"Utopias, Subtopias, Dystopias in the Novels of Anthony Burgess"
    K06
"Variations on an Antiheroic Theme" A29
"Verdicts of Guilty" A31
Vision Obscured, The J11

"Wagnerian Affirmation: Anthony Burgess's The Worm and the Ring"
    L08
"Waugh and Anthony Burgess: Some Notes toward an Assessment of
    Influence and Affinities" L110
"What Shall We Do About Anthony Burgess?" A07, A22, L97
"Whistle a Tune from Thomas Mann" L123
"Who Said Good Books Make Bad Movies?" L38
Who's Who in Twentieth Century Literature J28
"Who's Your Agent?" A28
"Will the Real Shakespeare Please Stand Up?" D26
"William the Silent" D26
"Winners Weepers" A25
Word for World Is Forest, The K07
"Words, Words and More Words" A13
"Words, Words, Words" A21
World Literature Since 1945: Critical Surveys J18
"World Without Sex" A30
"Wortsampler" D07
"Wracks of Empire" A08
"Writing in Rome" L41
"Wry and Comic Novel, A" A26
"Zeffirelli to Direct a TV Life of Christ" L126

Abercomways, Christobel Lady
G77
Across the Sea Wall G395
Adler, Larry G15
Adventures of Augie March, The
G183
After Many a Summer G66
Alderson, William G301
Ali-Shah, Omar G137
Aluko, T. M. G70
Ambidextrous Universe, The
G48
Amis, Kingsley G05, G139,
G371
Anatomy of Melancholy G07
Anecdotal History of Old Times
in Singapore, An G73
Another Book About London G43
Anouilh, Jean G90
Ansky, Saul G123
Anti-Death League, The G139
Apes of God, The G218
Arendt, Hannah H01
Aristophanes G61
Armstrong, Sir Thomas G26
Art of James Joyce, The G79
Art of Rudyard Kipling, The
G193
Assistant, The G44
At the Piano G192
Attenborough, David G34
Auden, W. H. G21, G29, G312
Aussie English G389
Austen, Jane G47
Australian Language, The G11
Ayston, Michael G80

Bagehot, William G33
Baird, Thomas G310
Baker, Sidney G11
Baldwin, James G45, G145,

G407
Balloon Over the Alps G108
Barbirolli, Sir John G24
Bardach, Emilie G17
Barker, Dudley G231
Barnett, Lincoln G449
Barth, John G55, H02
Bartók, Béla G14
Barzun, Jacques G96
Bashford, Henry Howarth G30
Bates, H. E. G407
Bateson, F. W. G350
Baudelaire, Charles G25
Bawdy Bard G413
Beauty and the Beast G22
Becket, Saint Thomas G90
Beckett, Samuel G105, G245
Beckett at Sixty G245
Beethoven, Ludvig van G19,
G25, G140
Bell, Martin G390
Belli, Giuseppe Gioacchino
G472
Bellow, Saul G183, H02
Bennet, Arnold G231
Benstock, Bernard G118
Bentley, Nicholas G167
Bercouici, Leonarto G395
Berg, Alban G26
Bernart, Julian G24
Berne, Stanley G343
Berto, Giuseppe G78
Better Dead than Red G70
Big M, The G80
Birds, The G61
Bit Between My Teeth, The
G420
Black Candle for Mr. Gogarty,
A G66
Black Sun G59
Blades, James G329

Blasting and Bombadiering G146
Blodgett, Harold W. G138
Blom-Cooper, Lois G222
Bloomfield, Anthony G429
Blues for Mr. Charlie G45
Bolton, W. F. G295
Bonheim, Helmut G79
Bonnard, Georges A. G267
Boothby, (Lord) G26, G127
Borges, Jorge Luis G396
Boulle, Pierre G36
Bourquin, Paul G310
Bowen, John G395
Boy Who Wanted Peace, The G324
Bradley, John L. G82
Bradley, Sculley G138
Brahms, Johannes G22
Brahms, Carl G16
Braine, John H02
Brecht, Bertolt G15, G41
Breit, Harvey G100
Brendan Behan, Man and Show-
  man G469
Bridges, Anthony G98
British Folklorists, The G234
Britten, Benjamin G14, G15
Brod, Max G315
Brook, Peter G19
Brooke, Jocelyn G17
Brooke, Rupert G13
Brooks, Cleanth G21, G26
Brophy, Brigid G13, G81,
  G475
Brown, Ivor G144
Buck, Pearl H01
Buckley, Charles Burton G73
Buckley, William F. H09
Bunting, Charles T. H01
Burchfield, R. W. G232
Burnell, H. C. G338
Burnett, Hallie G407
Burnett, Whit G407
Burroughs, William G167,
  G297, G474
Burton, Robert G07
Buskers of Marrakesh, The
  G122
Butor, Michel H01
Butt, John G83

Caligula G151
Cambridge Hymnal, The G292

Cameron, John G73
Camus, Albert G53, G151
Carleton, V. B. G105
Carmichael, Joel G429
Carnets 1942-1951 G53
Carter, Sydney G90
Cary, Joyce G187
Catto, Max G395
Caught in the Web of Words
  G262
Cecil, David (Lord) G13
Changing English G197
Chekhov, Anton G41, G407
Chopin G22
Chou-En-lai G160
Christie, Agatha G261
Christopher Marlowe: His
  Life and Work G87
Churchill, Thomas H02
Churchill, Winston G19, G22
Clemons, Walter H03
Cleworth, J. G46
Clockwork Orange, A [Film]
  G51, G52, G60
Cloete, Stuart G324
Cockpit, The G310
Cocksure G131
Cohen, Morton G359
Cole, William G67
Collected Letters of Bernard
  Shaw G314
Collected Poems 1937-1966
  [Martin Bell] G390
Collected Short Stories [Robert
  Graves] G407
Collected Works of William
  Begehot, The G33
Collection Two [Frank O'Con-
  nor] G58
Comfort, Alex G02, G65
Company I've Kept, The G153
Company She Kept, The G414
Complete Plays of Bernard
  Shaw, The G427
Complete Poems [Gerard Man-
  ley Hopkins] G120
Complete Prefaces of Bernard
  Shaw, The G427
Connolly, Cyril G21
Connolly, Thomas G79
Conquest, Robert G371
Cool Meridian, The G70
Coppelia G20

Cornell, Louis L. G194
Corridors of Power G327
Cousteau, Jacques G156
Cradock, Fanny G16
Cradock, Johnny G16
Craft and Art of Dylan Thomas, The G241
Cronin, Anthony G105
Crosby, Caresse G15
Cudworth, Charles G373
Cullinan, John H04
Cutworth, Rene G32

Dahlberg, Edward G158
Daiches, David G26
Dalton, Jack B. G105
Damant, David G167
Dangling Man G183
Davis, Colin G17
Davis, Walter R. G376
Day, Robin G127
Dean, Winston G364
Deane, Peter G254
Dearden, James S. G50
Debussy, Claude G27
Defferre, Gaston G160
Degas, Edgar G80
DeLaurentiis, Dino G396
Desolation Angels G38
Destroyer, The G281
Defoe, Daniel H04
Diaries of Franz Kafka, The G315
Dick, Bernard G298
Dickson, Lovat G150
Dictionary of Cat Lovers, A G77
Dictionary of Slang, A G309
Dix, Carol H05, H06
Don Giovanni G15
Donleavy, J. P. G299
Donley, Michael G42
Don't Never Forget G475
Dorson, Richard M. G234
Dos Passos, John H04
Dr. Faustus G468
Drew, Philip G357
Drum Roll G329
Dubliners G392
Dunn, Nell G373
DuPré, Jacqueline G16
Durrell, Lawrence G89, H04
Dybbuk, The G123

Early English and Celtic Lyric, The G380
Edelhart, Mike H07
Edelstein, J. M. G472
Egyptologists, The G371
Ehrlich, A. W. H08
Elgar, Sir Edward G13, G16, G20, G396
Eliot, T. S. G21, G90, G196, H04
Ellman, Richard G366
Elsner, Gisela G429
Engeberg, Edward G57
England's People from Roman Occupation to the Present G294
Erotic Poetry G67
Essays by English and American Men of Letters, 1490-1839 G295
Eugene Onegin G340
Evans, Geraint G97
Exhumantions G54

Faber Book of Aphorisms, The G312
Face of Christ, The G98
Famous Tales of the Fantastic G407
Farley, Richard G22
Ferris, Paul G281
Fiction and the Reading Public G350
Fiedler, Leslie A. G67
Field, Bosworth G26
Fielding, Henry H04
Fielding, Xan G36
Fifty Works of English Literature We Could Do Without G81
Finnegans Wake G17, G105
Firebird, The G23
Firmage, George J. G241
First Folio of Shakespeare, The G84
Fiske, Roger G364
Fitzgerald, F. Scott H04
Fitzgibbon, Constance G241
Fixer, The G44
Flanders, Michael G90
Flaubert: The Making of the Master G12
Flaubert, Gustave G12, G106

Fleming, Gordon H.   G50
Fletcher, John   G428
Follet, William   G96
Fonteyn, Margot   G24
Ford, Ford Madox   H04
Forster, E. M.   H04
Forster, Malcolm   G187
Fowler's End   G49
Franco, Francisco   G71
Frayn, Michael   G113
Freund, Gisele   G105
Friedland, Zui   G123
Friedman, Alan   G300
Friel, George   G324
Friends and Heroes   G330
Friends in Low Places   G371
Frost, David   G128
Furbank, P. N.   G181
Fussell, B. H.   G104

Galbraith, Kenneth   G90
Galileo   G155
Games of Chance   G371
Gardner, Martin   G48
Garland for Dylan Thomas, A
   G241
Ghosts, The   G269
Giant Dwarfs, The   G429
Gibbon, Edward   G267
Gilbert, William S.   G16, G17
Gilden, K. R.   G330
Giles Goat-Boy   G55
Gilliatt, Penelope   G429
Gilmore, Maeve   G328
Girls in Their Married Bliss
   G70
Gladiators, The   G195
Glanville, Brian   G330
Gleneak, W.   G111
Goddard, Donald   G43
Götterdämmerung, Die   G27
Going to Meet the Man   G407
Golding, William   G68, G129,
   G316
Goldman, Arnold   G118
Goodall, Jane   G90
Goodman, Benny   G18
Graves, Robert   G137, G407
Gray, Alasdair   G21
Gray, Anthony   G330
Great Short Stories of the World
   G407
Green, Reuben   G127

Greene, Graham   G134, G135,
   G257, G322, G323, G453,
   H01, H04
Greenwood, Walter   G269
Grimm, Jacob   G142
Grimm, Wilhelm   G142
Grumbach, Doris   G414
Guide to English Literature, A
   G350

H. G. Wells--Journalism and
   Prophecy, 1893-1946   G102
Haggard, H. Rider   G359
Halebsky, N.   G169
Hamalian, Leo   G440
Hamlet   G28
Hamlyn, Paul   G427
Hanff, Helene   G85
Happy End   G62
Harris, Frank   G220
Harris, Wilson   G167
Harrison, George   G128
Harrison, John   G107
Hart, Clive   G105
Hartley, L. P.   G13
Hartnoll, Phyllis   G364
Harvey, Sir Paul   G130
Harwood, Johanna   G429
Hat of Authority, The   G310
Heat of the Sun, The   G217
Heinlein, Robert A.   G361
Hemingway, Ernest   H04
Henderson the Rain King   G183
Henry, P. L.   G380
Herbert, Alan (Sir)   G26
Heritage and Its History, A
   G190
Hermanas, Las   G23
Herzog   G183
Hicks, Jim   H10
Hidick, Wallace   G281
Highsmith, Patricia   G371
Hinde, Thomas   G371
Hingley, Ronald   G407
Hinman, Charlton   G84
His Turbulent Life and Times
   G150
Hitchcock, Alfred   G14
Hobson-Jobson   G338
Hobson's Choice   G62
Hogben, Lancelot   G260
Holbrook, David   G27, G292
Home, Sir Alec   G127

Honey Bird, The G324
Hooper, Walter G247
Hopkins, Gerard Manley G48,
    G120, G186
Horder, John H11
Hospitality of Miss Tolliver, The
    G407
Hot Gales, The G129
Hotchner, A. E. G147
Hotson, Leslie H01
Howard, Elizabeth Jane G155
Hughes, Douglas A. G457
Hughes, Ted G13
Hurry Sundown G330
Huxley, Aldous G66

"I Love Chairman Mao" G160
Ibsen, Henrik G17
In Pursuit of Music G192
Incubus (Male Oscuro) G78
Infirm Glory, The G40, G48
Inheritors, The G68
Inside Mr. Enderby G476
Iolanthe G17
Irving, Clifford G330
Isherwood, Christopher G54,
    G152
Italian Girl, The G175
Italo Svevo G181
Iyengar, Shri G145

Jacobsen, Josephine G94
James Boswell--The Earlier
    Years, 1740-1769 G39
James Joyce in Paris: His
    Final Years G105
James Murray and the Oxford
    English Dictionary G262
Janssen, Otto G179, G337
Jeffares, A. Norman G57
Jeffs, Rae G469
Jennings, Gary G449
Jesus of Nazareth G133, G304
Johnson, B. S. H01
Johnson, Paul G294
Johnson, Philip G20
Johnson, S. L. G169
Johnson, Samuel G140, G185
Jones, David G24
Josephs, Wilfred G21
Joyce, James G25, G79, G105,
    G161, G186, G188, G351,
    G366, G392, H01, H02, H04

Joyce Cary G187
Joyce Paradox, The G118
Joyce-Again's Wake G118
Joyce's Benefictions G79
Joyce's Portrait: Criticisms
    and Critiques G79
Juke Box Jury G17

Kafka, Franz G315
Kahn, Herman G48, G408
Kaliyuga G343
Kangaroo G68
Karp, David H01
Karp, Walter G103
Kazakov, Yury G407
Kell, Joseph G321, G476,
    H02, H10
Kermode, Frank H01
Kerouac, Jack G38
Kersh, Gerald G49, G407
Kesey, Ken H02
Kilpatrick, Sarah G70
Kipling, Rudyard G186, G194,
    G359
Kipling in India G194
Kitchen Party G16
Klee, Robert G16
Klemperer, Otto G19
Knebel, Fletcher G330
Koch, Christopher G395
Koestler, Arthur G195
Kops, Bernard G281
Koun, Karolos G61
Krebs, Albin H12
Kronemeyer, Warren G298
Kronenberger, Louis G312
Khrushchev, Nikita G151
Krutch, Joseph Wood G92
Kubrick, Stanley G51, G52,
    G60, H06

Lacey, Robert G170
Lady Windemere's Fan G128
Langley, Noel G49
Language and Silence G387
Language of the Law, The
    G222
Larkin, Philip G20
Last Exit to Brooklyn G269,
    G457
Late Call G327
Laundresses, The G80
Laurent, Yves St. G03

Law Unto Themselves, A   G35
Lawrence, D. H.   G68
Lawrence, Dan   G314
Lear, Evelyn   G25
Leaves of Grass   G138
Leavis, Q. D.   G350
Lennon, John   G128
Letters of James Joyce, Vols.
   II and III   G366
Letters of Malcolm Lowry, The
   G100
Levey, Michael   G81
Levi-Strauss, Claude   G20, G48,
   G72, G166, H02
Levy, John   G24
Lewis, Anthony   H13
Lewis, C. S.   G274
Lewis, Wyndham   G146, G218
Literary Guide to Seduction, A
   G67
Literary Life, The   G254
Little Learning, A: The First
   Volume of an Autobiography
   G450
Litz, A. Walton   G79
Lives of the Poets   G185
Livings, Henry   G24
Llewellyn, Richard   G371
Lord of the Flies   G68, G316
Love from Venus   G395
Love on the Dock   G269
Lowell, Robert   G24
Lowry, Malcolm   G100
Lowry, Margerie Bonner   G100
Lunch with Ashurbanipal   G281
Lutyens, Mary   G50

McCauley, Rose   G311
McCormick, Anne H.   G10,
   G204
MacDiarmid, Hugh   G153
Mackenzie, Robert   G127
Maclean, A. D.   G407
McLuhan, Marshall   G66, G92,
   G255
MacMillan, Kenneth   G23
Magdalene   G388
Magi and the Commisar, The
   G195
Magic Flute, The   G17
Maharshi Silent Song   G128
Mailer, Norman   G26
Main Experiment, The   G70

Majesty   G170
Making of a Publisher, The
   G307
Malamud, Bernard   G44
Malcolm X   G145
Malko, George   H14
Mallabee   G310
Man Alive: No Fixed Abode
   G66
Manheim, Ralph   G324
Mann, Thomas   G468, H04
Manning, Mrs. R. N.   G169
Manning, Olivia   G330
Manningham, John   G168
Mao Tse-tung   G410
Marat-Sade   G19
Mare, Walter de la   G422
Marschner, Wolfgang   G26
Mary, Queen of England   G128
Matthews, Denis   G25, G192
Maugham, W. Somerset   G473
May We Borrow Your Husband?
   G257
Meeting, A   G152
Meister, Robert   G67
Meistersinger, Die   G22
Memoirs of a Malayan Official,
   The   G221
Memoirs of My Life   G267
Menuhin, Yehudi   G17, G20,
   G24, G145, G446
Mexico's Day of the Dead
   G396
Michelangelo   G155, G251
Milic, Louis   G04
Millais and the Ruskins   G50
Miller, Henry   G282
Miller, Jonathan   G19, G26
Milton, John   G253
Miss MacIntosh, My Darling
   G425
Mitchell, Julian   G190
Modern American Usage   G96
Modern Tragedy   G431
Moguilevsky, Eugene   G14
Moment and Other Pieces, The
   G56
Monkey Watches, The   G395
Montemore, Mike   G298
Moore, Henry   G21
Morgan, Edwin   G472
Morley, Robert   G156
Morley, Sheldon   H15

Morris, Ivan G182
Morris, James G317
Morris, Johnny G32
Mother Courage G41
Mother Goose G88
Mother Tongue, The G260
Mots d'Heures G115
Moynihan, William T. G241
Mozart, Wolfgang Amadeus
  G17, G18
Mueller, William R. G94
Muggeridge, Malcolm G26
Multiple Modern God and Other
  Stories, The G343
Murdoch, Iris G68, G175
Murphy, Robert G429
Murray, James G262
Murray, K. M. Elisabeth G262
Murray, Patrick G253
My Fair Lady G164
My Life and Loves G220
My Life and Times G282

Nabokov, Vladimir G319, G335,
  G340, H01, H02, H04
Naked Lunch, The G297
Napoleon G140, H01
Nature and Human Nature G65
Nefertiti G429
New Approach to Joyce, A G79
New Canon of English Poetry,
  A G37
New English Bible G90, G258
New Life, A G44
Newton, Ivor G192
Nicholson, Hubert G310
Nicholson, "Lord Chief Daron"
  G82
Night in Lisbon, The G324
Night of Camp David G330
Nineteenth Century Minor Poets
  G29
Nkrumah, Kwame G136
No's Knife G245
Nova Express G474
Novel and Society, The G379
Novels of Samuel Beckett, The
  G428
November G106
Nuffield, (Lord) G145
Numquam G89
Nureyev, Rudolf G24

O Canada G99
O'Brien, Edna G70
O'Brien, Flann G392
O'Conner, Frank G58
O'Donovan, Patrick G90,
  G136
Oedipus G166
Of Other Worlds: Essays and
  Stories by C. S. Lewis
  G247
O'Faolain, Sean G217
O'Grady, John G389
Oliver, Wendy G269
Oliver Twist G83
One Hand Clapping G16
One Man, One Matchet G70
Onions, C. T. G248
Ornithes G61
Orwell, George G02, G162,
  H01
Osborn, James M. G06
Osborne, Charles G81
O'Toole, Peter G28
"Our Bumper Harvest" G160
"Our Communal Dining-Hall"
  G160
Our Tropical Possessions in
  Malayan India G73
Owe by Owen G429
Owen, Wilfred G15
Oxford Companion to English
  Literature, The G130
Oxford Dictionary of English
  Etymology, The G248
Oxford English Dictionary
  G232
Oxford Revue, The G98

Page 2 G323
Painting as a Pastime G19
Panorama G412
Papa Hemingway G147
Parkinson, C. Northcote G35
Partridge, A. C. G197
Partridge, Eric G309
Patterns of Three and Four
  G310
Pei, Mario G141
Penetrators, The G330
Personalities of Language G449
Perspectives on Pornography
  G457
Perutz, Kathryn G269

Phelps, Robert   G254
Pillow Book of Sei Shonagun,
  The   G182
Places   G317
Plant, Wilson   G167
Plaster Bed, The   G324
Pleasure of Ruins   G311
Plumed Serpent, The   G68
Podro, Michael   G25
Poems of Gerard Manley Hop-
  kins   G48
Poets Through Their Letters
  G320
Polnay, Peter de   G324
Pond, The   G429
Pope John   G136
Porter, Horace   G265
Portrait of a Queen   G45
Poston, Elizabeth   G292
Potter, Dennis   G86
Potter, Simeon   G197
Pottle, Frederick A.   G39, G262
Powdered Eggs   G281
Powell, Anthony   H02
Powell, Lester   G80
Price, Alan   G95
Priestly, J. B.   G56
Prisoner, The   G66
Pritchard, K.   H17
Pritchett, V. S.   G117
Professor, The   G50
Profumo, John Dennis   G32
Prokofiev, Sergei Sergeyevich   G24
Proud African, The   G136
Purcell, Victor   G221
Pushkin, Aleksandr   G340
Pygmalion   G164
Pynchon, Thomas   H01

Quest Under Capricorn   G34
Question of Modernity, A   G105

Rachmaninov, Sergei Vassilie-
  vich   G14
Random House Dictionary of
  the English Language, The
  G96
Ratcliffe, Michael   G407
Raven, Simon   G345, G371
Raw and the Cooked, The   G72
Reactionaries   G107
Rebanks, L.   G169
Reeve, Ada   G160

Reilly, Lemuel   H18
Remarque, Erich Maria   G324
Renault, Mary   H04
Reynolds, Stanley   G70
Richler, Mordecai   G131
Riemer, G.   H19
"The Ring" ... A Number of
  Interpretations. "   G447
Robbe-Grillet, Alain   G269
Robert Browning: A Collection
  of Critical Essays   G357
Robinson, Robert   H20
Rogue's Progress: An Auto-
  biography of 'Lord Chief
  Daron' Nicholson   G82
Roman Summer   G23
Romeo and Juliet   G24
Rooten, Luis Dantin van   G115
Rossetti, Dante Gabriel   G50
Rossetti and the Pre-Raphaelite
  Brotherhood   G50
Rostand, Edmond   H04
Rostropovich, Mstislav   G14,
  G16, G18
Rota, Vassilis   G61
Roth, Philip   H02
Rowse, A. L.   G87, H01
Royal Foundation and Other
  Plays   G345
Rubaiyat of Omar Khayyam,
  The   G137
Rudyard Kipling   G194, G359
Rudyard Kipling to Rider Hag-
  gard   G359
Ruskin, John   G50
Russo, William   G396
Ryf, Robert S.   G79

Sade, Marquis de   G303
Safer, Morley   G80
Saint's Day   G41
Salinger, J. D.   H04
Sanders, Dr. Kingsley   G189
Sanders, John   G310
Sargent, Malcolm (Sir)   G26
Sarrute, Nathalie   H01
Sassoon, Siegfried   G199
Satyr and the Saint, The
  G395
Sauveur, F. St.   G143
Sayers, Dorothy   G26
Schrank, Joseph   G282
Schumann cello concerto   G16

Scope of Anthropology, The
  G48, G166
Scott, Sir Walter G47
Second Home, A G330
Secret Laughter G422
Seize the Day G183
Selby, Hubert, Jr. G269, G457,
  H02
Selected Letters of Dylan
  Thomas G241
Severed Head, A G68
Severn, Arthur G50
Sexual Cycle of Human Warfare,
  The G49
Seymour-Smith Martin G320
Shakespeare G16, G20, G26,
  G168, G180, G364, G413,
  H01
Shakespeare and Music G26
Shakespeare in Music: A Col-
  lection of Essays G364
Shakespeare's Bawdy G309
Shaw George Bernard G144,
  G164, G315, G427
Shaw, Robert G24
Shaw in His Time G144
Shea, George W. G440
Sheba's Landing G310
Shonagun, Sei G182
Siegfried Sassoon: A Critical
  Story G199
Sillitoe, Allan H02
Simenon, Georges H04
Simmons, Charles G281
Singular Man, A G299
Skinner, B. F. G103, H01
Slaughter, Carolyn G388
Smell of Bread, The G407
Smith, Stevie G25
Snapshots: Towards a New
  Novel G269
Snow, C. P. G327
Solid Gold Cadillac, The G45
Solid Mandala, The G425
Solti, Georg G14
Sontag, Susan G20
Source of the River Kwai, The
  G36
Spare the Rod and Spoil the
  Writer G21
Speak, Memory G319
Spearman, Diana G379
Spence, Joseph G06

Spender, Stephen G67
Stacton, David G343
Starkie, Enid G12
Steiner, George G387
Sterling, Mrs. G15
Stevens, John G364
Stewart, J. I. M. G194
Stewart, Thomas G25
Stone, Brian G440
Stories, 1895-1897 (Anton
  Chekhov) G407
Story of Language, The
  G141
Stowe, Harriet Beecher
  G239
Strike the Father Dead G468
Styron, William H02
Sullivan, Arthur S. G16, G17
Suspension of Mercy, A G371
Swann, Donald G90
Swann, Nancy G85
Sweet Morn of Judas' Day
  G371
Synge, J. M., Collected Works
  By G95

Take It or Leave It G18
Talking to Women G373
Taub, Sheila G85
Taylor, Allan G34
Tennyson, Alfred Lord G98
Testament of Samuel Beckett,
  The G94
Thal, Herbert van G407
There Goes Davey Cohen G269
There's a Porpoise Close Be-
  hind Us G49
Thieves in the Night G195
Third Girl G261
Third Policeman, The G392
38th Floor, The G330
Thody, Phillip G53
Thomas, Dylan G241
Thorpe, Michael G199
Thoughts G410
Three Sisters, The G41
Throw G429
Thundy, Zacharias G170
Tillotson, Kathleen G83
Time Is G24
Tin Men, The G113
Tippett, Michael G19, G21
Toccata G13

Told by an Idiot   G311
Tompkins, J. M. S.   G193
Tonight   G412
Tortelier, Paul   G13, G14, G25
Towers of Trebizond, The   G311
Towers, Robert   G395
Traviata, La   G13
Treasure of Our Tongue, The   G449
Tregor, Charles   G16
Trevor, William   G25
Tucker, Rex   G66
Tudor to Augustan English   G197
Turn of the Novel, The   G300
Twelve and a Tilly   G105
Two Old Ladies   G15

Ulysses   G161, G259, G351
Umans, Robert   G291
Uncle Tom's Cabin   G239
Unconventional English from the Fifteenth Century   G309
Under the Volcano   G100
Unfinished Journey   G446
Updike, John   G198, H01
Ure, Peter   G57

Vast Design: Patterns in W. B. Yeats' Aesthetic, The   G57
Velvet Bubble, The   G269
Verdi, Giuseppe   G23
Victim, The   G183
Vidal, Nicole   G429
Voices 2   G407

W. B. Yeats: Selected Criticism   G57
Wagar, W. Warren   G102
Wagner, Richard   G27, G447
Wain, John   G468
Waldo, D. E.   G104
Walker, David   G310
Walker, Keith   G262
Wallace, Irving   G259
Walters, Norman   G49
Walton, Sir William   G97
War Requiem   G15
Wars of the Roses   G26
Waterhouse, Keith   H02

Waugh, Evelyn   G101, G155, G450, H02, H04
Wedding Party, The   G407
Weightman, Doreen   G72
Weightman, John   G72
Weiner, Anthony   G408
Welles, Orson   G28
Wells, Doreen   G22
Wells, H. G.   G47, G102, G150
Wescott, Roger   G92
Weybright, Victor   G307
Wheatley, Dennis   G13
Where the Buffalo Roams   G86
Whicker, Alan   G160
White, Patrick   G425
White, Wilfred Hyde   G156
Whiting   G41
Whitman, Walt   G138
Williams, Christopher Hodder   G70
Williams, Oscar   G241
Williams, Raymond   G431
Wilson, Angus   G327
Wilson, Edmund   G99, G420
Wilson, Harold   G382
Winn, Godfrey   G40, G48
Winter Tales 11   G407
Winter, Alice   G269
Wolff, Geoffrey   G59
Woods, John A.   G239
Working Novelist, The   G117
Works of Thomas Campion, The   G376
World Away, A: A Memoir of Mervyn Peake   G328
World Elsewhere, A   G395
Wright, Barbara   G269
Writer by Trade   G231
Writer's World   G13

Year 2000, The   G408
Yeats, W. B.   G57, G90
Yeomen of the Guard, The   G16
Yes from No-Man's Land   G281
Young, Marguerite   G425
Yule, Henry   G338

Zeffirelli, Franco   G133